THE PELICAN SHAKESPEARE
GENERAL EDITOR : ALFRED HARBAGE
AB14
KING LEAR

WILLIAM SHAKESPEARE

The Tragedy of King Lear

EDITED BY

ALFRED HARBAGE

PENGUIN BOOKS

BALTIMORE · MARYLAND

This edition first published 1958
Reprinted July 1960
PENGUIN BOOKS INC.
3300 Clipper Mill Road, Baltimore 11, Maryland

[*Educational Representative: D. C. Heath & Co.*
285 Columbus Avenue, Boston 16, Mass.]

Printed in the United States of America

CONTENTS

Shakespeare and His Stage   7

The Texts of the Plays   12

Introduction   15

King Lear   33

Appendix: The Quarto Text   173

SHAKESPEARE AND HIS STAGE

William Shakespeare was christened in Holy Trinity Church, Stratford-on-Avon, April 26, 1564. His birth is traditionally assigned to April 23rd. He was the eldest of four boys and two girls who survived infancy in the family of John Shakespeare, glover and trader of Henley Street, and his wife Mary Arden, daughter of a small landowner of Wilmcote. In 1568 John was elected Bailiff (equivalent to Mayor) of Stratford, having already filled the minor municipal offices. The town maintained for the sons of the burgesses a free school, taught by a university graduate and offering preparation in Latin sufficient for university entrance; its early registers are lost, but there can be little doubt that Shakespeare received the formal part of his education in this school.

On November 27, 1582, a license was issued for the marriage of William Shakespeare (aged eighteen) and Ann Hathaway (aged twenty-six), and on May 26, 1583, their child Susanna was christened in Holy Trinity Church. The inference that the marriage was forced upon the youth is natural but not inevitable; betrothal was legally binding at the time, and was sometimes regarded as conferring conjugal rights. Two additional children of the marriage, the twins Hamnet and Judith, were christened on February 2, 1585. Meanwhile the prosperity of the elder Shakespeares had declined, and William was impelled to seek a career outside Stratford.

The tradition that he spent some time as a country teacher is old but unverifiable. Because of the absence of records his early twenties are called the "lost years," and only one thing about them is certain — that at least some of these years were spent in winning a place in the acting profession. He may have begun as a provincial trouper, but by 1592 he was established in London and prominent enough to be attacked. In a pamphlet of that year, *Groatsworth of Wit*, the ailing Robert Greene complained of the neglect which university writers like himself had suffered from actors, one of whom was daring to set up as a playwright:

> ... an upstart crow beautified with our feathers, that with his *Tiger's heart wrapt in a player's hide* supposes he is as well able to bombast out a blank verse as the best of you, and being an absolute Johannes-factotum, is in his own conceit the only Shake-scene in a country.

The pun on his name, and the parody of his line "O tiger's heart wrapt in a woman's hide" (*III Henry VI*), pointed clearly to Shakespeare. Some of his admirers protested, and Henry Chettle, the editor of Greene's pamphlet, saw fit to apologize:

> I am as sorry as if the original fault had been my fault, because myself have seen his demeanor no less civil than he excellent in the quality he professes. Besides divers of worship have reported his uprightness of dealing, which argues his honesty, and his facetious grace in writing that approves his art. (Prefatory epistle, *Kind Heart's Dream*)

The plague closed the London theatres for many months in 1593–94, denying the actors their livelihood. To this period belong Shakespeare's two narrative poems, *Venus and Adonis* and *Rape of Lucrece*, both dedicated to the Earl of Southampton. No doubt the poet was rewarded with a gift of money as usual in such cases, but he did no further dedicating and we have no reliable information on whether Southampton, or anyone else, became his regular patron. His sonnets, first mentioned in 1598 and published without his consent in 1609, are intimate without being explicitly autobiographical. They seem to commemorate the poet's friendship with an idealized youth, rivalry with a more favored poet, and love affair with a dark mistress; and his bitterness when the mistress betrays him in conjunction with the friend; but it is difficult to decide precisely what the "story" is, impossible to decide whether it is fictional or true. The real distinction of the sonnets, at least of those not purely conventional, rests in the universality of the thoughts and moods they express, and in their poignancy and beauty.

In 1594 was formed the theatrical company known until 1603 as the Lord Chamberlain's Men, thereafter as the King's Men. Its original membership included, besides Shakespeare, the beloved clown Will Kempe and the famous actor Richard Burbage. The company acted in various London theatres and even toured the provinces, but it is chiefly associated in our minds with the Globe Theatre built on the south bank of the Thames in 1599. Shakespeare was an actor and joint owner of this company (and its Globe) through the remainder of his creative years. His plays, written at the average rate of two a year, together with Burbage's acting won it its place of leadership among the London companies.

Individual plays began to appear in print, in editions both honest and piratical, and the publishers became increasingly aware of the value of Shakespeare's name on the title pages. As early as 1598 he was hailed as the leading English dramatist in the *Palladis Tamia* of Francis Meres:

As Plautus and Seneca are accounted the best for Comedy and Tragedy among the Latins, so Shakespeare among the English is the most excellent in both kinds for the stage: for Comedy, witness his *Gentlemen of Verona*, his *Errors*, his *Love labors lost*, his *Love labors won [Taming of the Shrew?]*, his *Midsummers night dream*, & his *Merchant of Venice*; for Tragedy, his *Richard the 2*, *Richard the 3*, *Henry the 4*, *King John*, *Titus Andronicus*, and his *Romeo and Juliet*.

The note is valuable, both in indicating Shakespeare's prestige and in helping us to establish a chronology. In the second half of his writing career, history plays gave place to the great tragedies; and farces and light comedies gave place to the problem plays and symbolic romances. In 1623, seven years after his death, his former fellow actors, John Hemming and Henry Condell, cooperated with a group of London printers in bringing out his plays in collected form. The volume is generally known as the First Folio.

Shakespeare had never severed his relations with Stratford. His wife and children may sometimes have shared his London lodgings, but their home was Stratford. His son Hamnet was buried there in 1596, and his daughters Susanna and Judith were married there in 1607 and 1616 respectively. (His father, for whom he had secured a coat of arms and thus the privilege of writing himself gentleman, died in 1601, his mother in 1608.) His considerable earnings in London, as actor-sharer, part owner of the Globe, and playwright, were invested chiefly in Stratford property. In 1597 he purchased for £60 New Place, one of the two most imposing residences in the town. A number of other business transactions, as well as minor episodes in his career, have left documentary records. By 1611 he was in a position to retire, and he seems gradually to have withdrawn from theatrical activity in order to live in Stratford. In March, 1616, he made a will, leaving token bequests to Burbage, Hemming, and Condell, but the bulk of his estate to his family. The most famous feature of the will, the bequest of the second-best bed to his wife, reveals nothing about Shakespeare's marriage; the quaintness of the provision seems commonplace to those familiar with ancient testaments. Shakespeare died April 23, 1616, and was buried in the Stratford church where he had been christened. Within seven years a monument was erected to his memory on the north wall of the chancel. Its portrait bust and the Droeshout engraving on the title page of the First Folio provide the only likenesses with an established claim to authenticity. The best verbal vignette was written by his rival Ben Jonson, the more impressive for being imbedded in a context mainly critical:

> ... I loved the man, and do honor his memory (on this side idolatry) as much as any. He was indeed honest, and of an open and free nature: he had an excellent fancy, brave notions, and gentle expressions. ... (*Timber or Discoveries*, c. 1623–30)

The reader of Shakespeare's plays is aided by a general knowledge of the way in which they were staged. The King's Men acquired a roofed and artificially lighted theatre only toward the close of Shakespeare's career, and then only for winter use. Nearly all his plays were designed for performance in such structures as the Globe — a three-tiered amphitheatre with a large rectangular platform extending to the center of its yard. The plays were staged by daylight, by large casts brilliantly costumed, but with only a minimum of properties, without scenery, and quite possibly without intermissions. There was a rear stage balcony for action "above," and a curtained rear recess for "discoveries" and other special effects, but by far the major portion of any play was enacted upon the projecting platform, with episode following episode in swift succession, and with shifts of time and place signaled the audience only by the momentary clearing of the stage between the episodes. Information about the identity of the characters and, when necessary, about the time and place of the action was incorporated in the dialogue. No additional indications of place have been inserted in the present editions; these are apt to obscure the original fluidity of structure, with the emphasis upon action and speech rather than scenic background. The acting, including that of the youthful apprentices to the profession who performed the parts of women, was highly skillful, with a premium placed upon grace of gesture and beauty of diction. The audiences, a cross section of the general public, commonly numbered a thousand, sometimes more than two thousand. Judged by the type of plays they applauded, these audiences were not only large but also perceptive.

THE TEXTS OF THE PLAYS

About half of Shakespeare's plays appeared in print for the first time in the folio volume of 1623. The others had been published individually, usually in quarto volumes, during his lifetime or in the six years following his death. The copy used by the printers of the quartos varied greatly in merit, sometimes representing Shakespeare's true text, sometimes only a debased version of that text. The copy used by the printers of the folio also varied in merit, but was chosen with care. Since it consisted of the best available manuscripts, or the more acceptable quartos (although frequently in editions other than the first), or of quartos corrected by reference to manuscripts, we have good or reasonably good texts of most of the thirty-seven plays.

In the present series, the plays have been newly edited from quarto or folio texts depending, when a choice offered, upon which is now regarded by bibliographical specialists as the more authoritative. The ideal has been to reproduce the chosen texts with as few alterations as possible, beyond occasional relineation, expansion of abbreviations, and modernization of punctuation and spelling. Emendation is held to a minimum, and such material as has been added, in the way of stage directions and lines supplied by an alternative text, has been enclosed in square brackets.

None of the plays printed in Shakespeare's lifetime were divided into acts and scenes, and the inference is that the author's own manuscripts were not so divided. In the folio collection, some of the plays remained undivided, some were divided into acts, and some were divided into acts and scenes. During the eighteenth century all of the plays were divided into acts and scenes, and in the Cambridge edition of the mid-nineteenth century, from which the influential Globe text derived, this division was more or less regularized and the lines were numbered. Many useful works of reference employ the act-scene-line apparatus established by the Globe text.

Since the act-scene division thus established is obviously convenient, but is of very dubious authority so far as Shakespeare's own structural principles are concerned, or the original manner of staging his plays, a problem is presented to modern editors. In the present series the act-scene division of the Globe text is retained marginally, and may be viewed as a reference aid like the line numbering. A printer's ornament marks the points of division when these points have been determined by a cleared stage indicating a shift of time and place in the action of the play, or when no harm results from the editorial assumption that there is such a shift. However, at those points where the established division is clearly misleading – that is, where continuous action has been split up into separate "scenes" – the ornament is omitted and the distortion corrected. This mechanical expedient seemed the best means of combining utility and accuracy.

The General Editor.

INTRODUCTION

The play begins with a moment of prose "exposition," an idle conversation about the partition of a kingdom and the bastardy of a son. Its tone is casual, jocular, polite. The son responds decorously to a social introduction. The speakers are wearing familiar masks. It is then as if these murmurs by the portal subsided at the opening of some old but half-remembered ceremony. All is ritual — heralding trumpet, formal procession, symbolic objects in coronet and map, a sequence of arbitrary yet strangely predictable acts. What can be made of it? Why should that patriarch who wishes to yield up his power and possessions require of the receivers declarations of love? Why should that maiden who honestly loves him respond only with declarations of her love of honesty? No logical reasons appear — ritual is ritual, its logic its own. Prose is yielding to poetry, "realism" to reality. *King Lear* is not true. It is an allegory of truth.

That its truths are not literal is the first thing about it discerned by the budding critical faculty. Everything is initially *patterned* — this one making obvious errors which he obviously will rue, these others emerging as the good and the evil in almost geometrical symmetry, with the inevitable sisters-three, the two elder chosen though wicked, the younger rejected though virtuous. Surely these are childish things! A defense has been offered by Tolstoy, in his valedictory judgment that the only truths conveyable in literature can be conveyed in the simplest folk-tale. But *King Lear* is not simple, and Tolstoy himself failed to see its relevance to his doctrine. Freud noticed its primitive features, and compared Goneril, Regan, and Cordelia to the caskets of lead, silver, and gold in *The Merchant of Venice*. He identified Cordelia as the benign, though resisted, call of death. Cordelia as the death-wish — *lovely and soothing death* — how suggestive this is! until we recognize that her identification as the life-wish might be equally suggestive. The value of such reflections lies in their reminder that the oldest story-patterns have the greatest power to touch off reverberations. No other framework than this parable-myth could have borne so well the weight of what Shakespeare was compelled to say.

The story of Lear and his three daughters was given written form four centuries before Shakespeare's birth. How much older its components may be we do not know. Cordelia in one guise or another, including Cinderella's, has figured in the folklore of most cultures, perhaps originally expressing what Emerson saw as the conviction of every human being of his worthiness to be loved and chosen, if only his *true* self were truly known. The figure of the ruler asking a question, often a riddle, with disastrous consequences to himself is equally old and dispersed. In his *Historia Regum Britanniae* (1136) Geoffrey of Monmouth converted folklore to history and established Lear and his daughters as rulers of ancient Britain, thus bequeathing them to the chronicles. Raphael Holinshed's (1587) declared that "Leir, the sonne of Baldud," came to the throne "in the year of the world 3105, at which time Joas reigned in Juda," but belief in the historicity of such British kings was now beginning to wane, and Shakespeare could deal freely with the record. He read the story also in John Higgins's lamentable verses in *A Mirrour for Magistrates* (1574), and in Edmund Spenser's *Faerie Queene*, II, 10,

27–32. He knew, and may even have acted in, a bland dramatic version, *The True Chronicle History of King Leir,* published anonymously in 1605 but staged at least as early as 1594.

The printing of the old play may mark an effort to capitalize upon the staging of Shakespeare's, performed at court on December 26, 1606, and probably first brought out at the Globe playhouse sometime in 1605, although its allusion to "these late eclipses of the sun and moon" was not necessarily suggested by those of September and October of that year. The only certain anterior limit of date is March 16, 1603, when Samuel Harsnett's *Declaration of Egregious Popishe Impostures* was registered for publication. That this excursion in "pseudo-demonology" was available to Shakespeare is evident in various ways, most clearly in the borrowed inventory of devils imbedded in Edgar's jargon as Tom o' Bedlam. It is of small consequence to fix the date of *King Lear* so far as its relation to the older play is concerned, which must be reckoned as analogue rather than source, but if, as seems certain, it was composed in 1605 or early 1606, it belongs to the same season of the poet's growth as *The Tragedy of Macbeth.*

In its pre-Shakespearean forms, both those mentioned above and others, the Lear story remains rudimentary. The emphasis may vary in various recensions, depending upon whether the author was most interested in the inexpedience of subdividing a kingdom, the mutability of fortune, or, as in the older play, the rewards of Christian virtue; but all are alike in that they end happily for Lear, who is reconciled to Cordelia and restored to his throne. The fact that the story was sometimes followed by a sequel in which Cordelia was finally hounded to suicide by the broodlings of her wicked sisters has little bearing on a remarkable fact: Shakespeare alone and in defiance of precedent conducted Lear to ultimate misery. *Enter Lear with Cordelia in his arms. . . . He dies.* These directions enclose a scene which demonstrates beyond any other in tragic literature the intransigence of poetic art – inventing the inevitable, investing horrifying things with beauty.

Compared with the tragedies of ancient Greece, and it is with these alone that one is tempted to compare it, *King Lear* suggests the Gothic order. Its form is irregular and organic, determined seemingly by a series of upward thrusts of mounting internal energy. There is even a Gothic element of the grotesque, as when mock-beggar, jester, and king, reduced to common condition, hold their mad juridical proceedings in a storm-lashed hovel, or when crazed king and blinded subject exchange lamentations and puns! In the method of Lear's madness there is often a savage humor, more remarkable when all is said than his companioning with a Fool. It was the Fool, however, who seemed to the next age the unpardonable sin against classical decorum. In the 1680 adaptation by Nahum Tate he was expunged from the play, along with the tragic ending. Tate capped the concluding felicities of the pre-Shakespearean versions by huddling up a marriage between Edgar and Cordelia; yet his work held the stage throughout the eighteenth century. It is always ruefully remarked that the greatest critic of the age approved the adaptation, but in fairness we should add that it was not for literary reasons. The pain of Shakespeare's concluding scenes was simply too much for Dr. Johnson; his response is preferable to that of those – fit for treasons, stratagems, and spoils – who can read these scenes unmoved.

The original play, or its approximation, was restored to the stage in the early nineteenth century, after it had begun to receive its critical due from the romantic essayists and poets. It is a poet's play. Keats saw in it the warrant for his conviction that truth and beauty are one, and, more surprisingly, recognized the choral and catalytic function of Lear's jester for the stroke of genius it was. Coleridge, Lamb, and Hazlitt also recorded illuminating judgments, and many critics since, of many different "schools," have said fine things about it.

The question now most frequently debated is whether the play is Christian and affirmative in spirit, or pagan and pessimistic. No work of art could endure the tugs of such a debate without being somewhat torn. "Pessimistic," like "optimistic," is a small word for a small thing, and *King Lear* is not small. It is sad, as all tragedies are sad. It is religious, as all great tragedies are religious. The exclusion of specific Christian reference, more consistent than in any other Shakespearean play of non-Christian setting, is in harmony with its Old Testament atmosphere ("when Joas ruled in Juda"), but it may reflect nothing more than evasion, in the printed text, of a recent Parliamentary ruling, which in effect labelled *God* in stage speech as blasphemy, *gods* as mere classical allusion. Although the play is rather inclusively than exclusively Christian, which can scarcely be deemed a fault, it shows obvious signs of its genesis in a Christian culture. To cite those involving a single character (other than Cordelia, who has often been viewed as a Christ-symbol), there is Edgar's persistence in returning good for evil, his preachments against the sin of despair, and his reluctance to kill except in trial by combat with its implied religious sanctions. Great questions are asked of the unseen powers — "Is there any cause in nature for these hard hearts?" — and these questions remain unanswered, but the silence which follows them should be viewed, here as in other contexts, as the substance of faith. On the human level, the implications of the play are more comforting than the data it abstracts. In our actual world, suffering is not always ennobling, evil not always self-consuming. In every scene where there is pain, there is someone who strives to relieve that pain. At the close, the merciless have all perished; the last sound we hear is the choral voices of the merciful.

The workers of evil are stylized in a way not quite typical of Shakespeare. He could not love these characters even as characters, except perhaps Edmund a little. To imitate the dominant animal imagery of the style, Cornwall is less repellent than Goneril and Regan only as the mad bull is less repellent than the hyena, they less repellent than Oswald only as the hyena is less repellent than the jackal. To the latter he failed to give even that engaging touch of the ludicrous he usually reserved for assistant villains. It is useless to speak of their "motivation." Like other aged parents Lear is no gift to good housewifery, and there is something poignantly familiar about such a one's trudging resentfully to the home of a second daughter. "Age is unnecessary." But to see a causal relationship between what he does to Goneril and Regan and what they do to him, or to interpret their aggression as normal revolt against parental domination, is simply to be perverse. The play deals directly, and in both its stories, with one indissoluble bond:

> We'll no more meet, no more see one another.
> But yet thou art my flesh, my blood, my daughter. . . .

Eroded, it leaves no human bond secure. To argue that Edmund's conduct is attributable to humiliating illegitimacy, we must supply him with an "unconscious" and

20

invoke its spectral evidence; there is no sign of sensitivity in his lines. Even that curious product of our times, the liberalism-gone-to-seed which automatically defends anything from treachery to sadism providing it savors of nonconformity, has found little to say for this insatiable quintet.

Shakespeare is not normally associated with hatred, but "a fierce hatred of cruelty and deceitful wickedness" informs *King Lear* – this the opinion of so pure an aesthetician as Benedetto Croce. Hazlitt has said, "It is then the best of all Shakespeare's plays, for it is the one in which he was most in earnest." A non-sequitur may lurk in this assertion, but we cannot deny its relevance. Our inescapable impression of the play is of its overwhelming sincerity. It says everything powerfully and everything twice – and always "what we feel, not what we ought to say." The language varies from the cryptic allusiveness of Lear's "mad" speeches to the biblical plainness of his pleas for forgiveness; and though it is often difficult, it is never ambiguous. Lamb has been much taken to task for declaring that "*Lear* is essentially impossible to be represented on a stage," but more often than not our experiences in the theatre confirm his view. There have been fine productions, but not very many: one touch of insincerity can rot everything away.

Those who now "introduce" this play must wish with Hazlitt, and with much more likelihood of greeting the wish of the reader, that they might resort to silence, since all that can be said will "fall short of the subject, or even what we ourselves conceive of it." Yet an effort must be made to state its theme, and to the present editor there seems no way of doing this except by focussing the gaze directly and continuously upon Lear himself.

"The King is coming." These words announce the first

entrance of the tragic hero. Let us see him as he is, no pre-
conceptions or critical rumors spoiling the innocence of our
vision. Nothing about him suggests infirmity or decay. His
magnitude and force are far greater than one's own. He
issues commands with the assurance of instinct and lifelong
custom. He holds a map in his hands like a Titan holding a
kingdom. The kingdom spreads before us in his spacious
utterance:

> Of all these bounds, even from this line to this,
> With shadowy forests and with champains riched,
> With plenteous rivers and wide-skirted meads,
> We make thee lady.

We make thee lady! Thus he disposes of a sector of the earth,
this ring-giver, this warrior-leader, this chosen one, his only
landlord God! Is it not passing fine . . . ? Here is no soft-
brained *Senex,* but the archetypal *King.*

As such Lear symbolizes Mankind, and we will say nothing essential about him by reckoning up his years and growing glib about the symptoms of senile dementia. The king-
figure surrogate is an understandable product of the human
mind in its early attempts at abstraction, since the most imposing of single men best lends his image to the difficult
concept of Man. His vicissitudes best epitomize the vicissitudes of all, since upon the highest altitude the sun shines
brightest and the cold snow lies most deep. Early Renaissance drama was steeped in the tradition of this symbolic figure, sometimes still called *King* as well as *Mankind, Everyman, Genus Humanum,* and the like. He is always
identifiable by his centrality in the action, and the mixed
company he keeps — vices or flatterers on the one hand,
virtues or truth-speakers on the other. And there stands

Lear – Goneril and Regan to the left, Kent and Cordelia to the right.

But this is also a family gathering. There is the father, and there the servant and children of his house. The central figure is, and seems always more so as the play weaves its spell, not only archetypal King, Man, and Father, but particular king, man, and father. No symbol that remained purely symbol could so touch our emotions. To have children of his flesh and blood, the father must be flesh and blood – such as can be old, grow weary, feel cold and wet.

Only a few days of fictional time elapse, only a few hours in the theatre, so that Lear's first words still echo in our ears as we hear his last.

> We make thee lady. . . . Let it be so, thy truth then be thy dower! . . . Peace, Kent! Come not between the dragon and his wrath. . . . The bow is bent and drawn; make from the shaft. . . . Therefore be gone. . . . Let me not stay a jot for dinner; go, get it ready. . . . Call the clotpoll back.

Such are Lear's accents at the beginning. And at the close –

> You must bear with me. . . . I am old and foolish. . . . Her voice was ever soft, gentle, and low. . . . Pray you undo this button. Thank you, sir.

He has learned a new language. We are required to accept this learning as good, but we are forbidden to rejoice.

The play is Lear's gethsemane, its great reality his suffering, which so draws us into itself that our conception of the work as a whole is formed in the crucible of our fear and pity. His anguish is kin with the anguish of Job, Prometheus, Oedipus, and other tragic projections of spirits in agony, but it retains its own peculiar quality. Its cause, its nature, and its meaning will always remain the imperfectly resolved crux of the play; and one can do no more than explain, with such confidence as one is able to muster, how these things appear to him.

To say that Lear gets what he deserves is to share the opinion of Goneril and Regan. (Some have even implied that Cordelia gets what she deserves, anaesthetizing their heads and hearts with obtuse moralisms suggested by the doctrine of "poetic justice.") What does Lear deserve? He is proud and peremptory, and it is better to be humble and temporizing, but there are occupational hazards in being a king, perhaps even in being a father. Is his charge not true that the world has lied to him, telling him he was wise before he was bearded, returning "yea and nay" to everything he said? His guilt is widely shared, and his "flaw" like that of Oedipus seems mysteriously hereditary. And it is linked inextricably with his virtues. We applaud the resurgence of youthful might that cuts down Cordelia's assassin. We admire the valor of his attempts (and they come quite early) to be patient, to compromise, to hold back womanish tears, to cling to his reason. Nothing is more moving than his bewildered attempts to meet "social" obligations as he kneels by Cordelia's body. We love his *manliness*. Pride has its value too.

Lear's errors stem from no corruption of heart. His rejection of Kent and Cordelia is the reflex of his attachment to them. The errors are not the man. The man is one who has valued and been valued by such as they. The things he wants – fidelity and love – are good things. That he should find them in his servant and his child seems to him an aspect of universal order. In his vocabulary, as distinct from Edmund's, such things are *natural*. His inability to dis-

24

tinguish between the false and the true, and his craving for visible displays, are not failings peculiar to him. "How much do you love me?" — few parents suppress this bullying question, spoken or unspoken, however much they may have felt its burden as children. It seems in the nature of some things that they always be learned too late, that as children we might have offered more, as parents demanded less. To punish a thankless child has the appearance of justice, to withdraw in one's age from the cares of state the appearance of wisdom, to dispose of one's goods by gift instead of testament the appearance of generosity. Plain men in their prime have been similarly deceived. Gloucester shakes his head sadly over Lear's injustice, folly, and selfishness as he duplicates his actions.

In the maimed but agile mind of the Fool faithfully dogging Lear's steps, his errors stand as an *idée fixe* and are harped upon with terrible iteration. We should not imitate the example. We may find more meaning in the excess of expiation. The purely physical suffering — denial of rest, exposure to wind and rain — is real, but it strikes the sufferer himself as little more than a metaphor. We may say that his spiritual suffering is in excess of his actual afflictions, that it is selfish and centrifugal, or a mere symptom of aged petulance, but if we do so, we are stopping our ears to the voice of Shakespeare and all his decent spokesmen. Lear's curse of Goneril is still alienating, like his treatment of Cordelia, but when he stands weeping before his cormorant daughters in whom he has put his faith, and they coolly and relentlessly strip him of every vestige of dignity, our hearts turn over. Humility may be good, but this humiliation is evil.

There is no *need* that this man be attended by a hundred knights, that his messenger be deferentially treated, or that his children offer him more than subsistence. His cause rests upon no more rational grounds than our powers of sympathy and imagination. "O reason not the need." As his every expectation is brutally defeated, and he looks in dazed recognition upon the world as it is instead of what he thought it was, of himself as he is instead of what he thought he was, we defer to his past illusions. He had never identified prestige merely as power, had never imagined that the visages of respect, kindliness, and love could contort into the hideous lines of icy contempt and sour indifference.

Lear's anguish now represents for us Man's horror and sense of helplessness at the discovery of evil – the infiltration of animality in the human world, naked cruelty and appetite. It is a fissure that threatens to widen infinitely, and we see Lear at the center of turbulence as it works its breakage in minds, in families, in nations, in the heavens themselves, interacting in dreadful concatenation.

The significance of Lear's response to his discovery is best seen in the light of Gloucester's. In Sidney's *Arcadia*, II, 10, the "storie of the Paphlagonian unkind King and his kinde sonne" repeats in essence the Lear legend, except that the children, false and true, are sons instead of daughters. By reducing the rank of Sidney's king and interweaving his parallel fate in alternate scenes, Shakespeare is able, amazingly, both further to universalize and further to particularize the experience of Lear. Gloucester also represents Man, but his distinction from Lear suggests the distinction between ordinary and extraordinary men. Gloucester is amiably confused about the tawdriness of his past, of which Edmund is the product, and sentimentally fumbling in the present. What appears in Lear as heroic error appears in him as gullibility. His fine moments are identical with those of a nameless serf of Cornwall's and an ancient tenant of his own — in the presence of cruelty he becomes kind and brave:

> *Gloucester*. I am tied to th' stake, and I must stand the course.
> *Regan*. Wherefore to Dover?
> *Gloucester*. Because I would not see thy cruel nails
> Pluck out his poor old eyes.

Like Lear he is incorrupt of heart, and he grows in dignity, but his total response to vicious encroachment is something akin to apathy and surrender; his instinct is to retreat.

Not so with Lear. He batters himself to pieces against the fact of evil. Granted that its disruptive power has been unleashed by his own error, so that error itself partakes of evil, as he is shudderingly aware, yet he remains the great antagonist. Falsity, cruelty, injustice, corruption — their appalling forms swirl about him in phantasmic patterns. His instinct is to rip them from the universe, to annihilate all things if it is the only way to annihilate these things. His charges of universal hypocrisy: "handy-dandy, which is the justice, which is the thief?" — his denial of human responsibility: "None does offend, none — I say none!" — his indictment of life itself:

> Thou know'st, the first time that we smell the air
> We wawl and cry —

cancel their own nihilism, because they sound no acquiescence. Lear is the voice of protest. The grandeur of his spirit supplies the impotence of his body as he opposes to evil all that is left him to oppose — his molten indignation, his huge invectives, his capacity for feeling pain.

This quality of Lear seen in retrospect, his hunger after righteousness, gives magnitude to the concluding scenes.

His spirit has been doubly lacerated by his own sense of guilt. He has failed "poor naked wretches" no different from himself, and he has wronged Cordelia. His remorse has found expression only in brief occasional utterances, welling up as it were against desperate efforts of containment, but its scalding power is revealed in his acts of abasement when he and Cordelia meet. The final episodes are all vitally linked. When the two are led in captive, we are made to look back upon their reunion, which he dreams of endlessly reenacting:

> When thou dost ask me blessing, I'll kneel down
> And ask of thee forgiveness;

then forward to their death:

> Upon such sacrifices, my Cordelia,
> The gods themselves throw incense.

The words help to effect that perfect coalescence of particular and general tragic experience achieved as he kneels beside her body. This is a father and his child who will come no more, the father remembering his own unkindness and the child's endearing ways. There is no melioration in his dying delusion that she still lives, no mention of an after-life. It is unspeakably sad. But it merges with a larger yet less devastating sadness. This is also a sacrifice, and although the somber tones of the survivors as they take up the burden of survival give it relevance to the future as well as the past, it is such a sacrifice as obliquely vindicates the gods if upon it they throw incense.

We know, not as an item of faith but of simple demonstrable fact, that we are greatly indebted for such wisdom as we have, that it was bought with "sacrifices." In the struggle of our kind against brutality, the great casualties, spiritual and even physical, have always been among those who have been best and those who have cared most. In the world of this play Cordelia has brought us the truest sense of human goodness, her words "No cause, no cause" the truest sense of moral beauty. She is the perfect offering. And so is Lear. She is best. He cares most for what is best. The play ends as it begins in an allegorical grouping, commemorating humanity's long, agonized, and continuing struggle to be human. This larger meaning gives our tears the dignity of an act of ratification and gratitude: to these still figures we have pitied we owe the gift of feeling pity.

Harvard University   ALFRED HARBAGE

Note on the text: In 1608 a version of *King Lear* appeared in a quarto volume sold by Nathaniel Butter at his shop at the Pied Bull. Its text was reproduced in 1619 in a quarto falsely dated 1608. Various theories have been offered to explain the nature of the Pied Bull text, the most recent being that it represents Shakespeare's rough draft carelessly copied, and corrupted by the faulty memories of actors who were party to the copying. In 1623 a greatly improved though "cut" version of the play appeared in the First Folio, evidently printed from the quarto after it had been carefully collated with the official playhouse manuscript. The present edition follows the folio text, and although it adds in square brackets the passages appearing only in the quarto, and accepts fifty-two quarto readings, it follows the chosen text more closely than do most recent editions. However, deference to the quarto is paid in an appendix, where its alternative readings, both those accepted and those rejected, are listed. Few editorial emendations have been retained, but see I, ii, 21 *top* (Q & F 'to'), II, ii, 138 *contemnèd'st* (Q 'temnest'), III, vi, 25 *bourn* (Q 'broom'), III, vi, 67 *lym* (Q & F 'him'), IV, ii, 57 *to threat* (Q 'threat'), IV, iii, 31 *moistened* (Q 'moistened her'). The quarto text is not divided into acts and scenes. The act and scene division here supplied marginally is that of the Globe edition, which in turn is that of the folio except that Act II, Scene ii of the latter has been subdivided into Scenes ii, iii, and iv. The continuity of the action here, and at several other misleadingly divided sections of the play, is indicated in the manner explained in the general foreword.

The Tragedy of
King Lear

[Names of the Actors

Lear, King of Britain
King of France
Duke of Burgundy
Duke of Cornwall
Duke of Albany
Earl of Kent
Earl of Gloucester
Edgar, son to Gloucester
Edmund, bastard son to Gloucester
Curan, a courtier
Old Man, tenant to Gloucester
Doctor
Lear's Fool
Oswald, steward to Goneril
A Captain under Edmund's command
Gentlemen
A Herald
Servants to Cornwall
Goneril ⎫
Regan ⎬ *daughters to Lear*
Cordelia ⎭
Knights attending on Lear, Officers, Messengers, Soldiers, Attendants

Scene
Britain]

Enter Kent, Gloucester, and Edmund.   I, i

Kent. I thought the King had more affected the Duke of
Albany than Cornwall.

Gloucester. It did always seem so to us; but now, in the division of the kingdom, it appears not which of the dukes
he values most, for equalities are so weighed that curiosity 5
in neither can make choice of either's moiety.

Kent. Is not this your son, my lord?

Gloucester. His breeding, sir, hath been at my charge. I have
so often blushed to acknowledge him that now I am
brazed to't.   10

Kent. I cannot conceive you.

Gloucester. Sir, this young fellow's mother could; where-
upon she grew round-wombed, and had indeed, sir, a son
for her cradle ere she had a husband for her bed. Do you
smell a fault?   15

Kent. I cannot wish the fault undone, the issue of it being
so proper.

Gloucester. But I have a son, sir, by order of law, some year
elder than this who yet is no dearer in my account:

I, i, 1 *affected* warmly regarded 2 *Albany* i.e. Scotland (once ruled by
'Albanacte') 5 *equalities . . . weighed* i.e. the portions weigh so equally
5–6 *curiosity . . . moiety* careful analysis by neither can make him prefer the
other's portion 8 *breeding* rearing 10 *brazed* brazened 11 *conceive* understand (with pun following) 17 *proper* handsome 19 *account* estimation

20   though this knave came something saucily to the world
       before he was sent for, yet was his mother fair, there was
       good sport at his making, and the whoreson must be
       acknowledged. Do you know this noble gentleman,
       Edmund?
25 *Edmund.* No, my lord.
   Gloucester. My Lord of Kent. Remember him hereafter as
       my honorable friend.
   Edmund. My services to your lordship.
   Kent. I must love you, and sue to know you better.
30 *Edmund.* Sir, I shall study deserving.
   Gloucester. He hath been out nine years, and away he shall
       again.   *[Sound a] sennet.*
       The King is coming.

       Enter [one bearing a coronet, then] King Lear, [then the
       Dukes of] Cornwall [and] Albany, [next] Goneril,
       Regan, Cordelia, and Attendants.

   Lear. Attend the lords of France and Burgundy, Gloucester.
35 *Gloucester.* I shall, my lord.   *Exit [with Edmund].*
   Lear. Meantime we shall express our darker purpose.
       Give me the map there. Know that we have divided
       In three our kingdom; and 'tis our fast intent
       To shake all cares and business from our age,
40   Conferring them on younger strengths while we
       Unburdened crawl toward death. Our son of Cornwall,
       And you our no less loving son of Albany,
       We have this hour a constant will to publish

---

20 *saucily* (1) impertinently (2) bawdily 22 *whoreson* (affectionate abuse,
but literally applicable, like 'knave' above) 31 *out* away (for training,
or in military service) 32 s.d. *sennet* trumpet flourish (heralding a procession) 36 *darker purpose* more secret intention (to require declarations
of affection) 38 *fast* firm 43 *constant . . . publish* fixed intention to announce

34

Our daughters' several dowers, that future strife
May be prevented now. The princes, France and Bur-
    gundy,   45
Great rivals in our youngest daughter's love,
Long in our court have made their amorous sojourn,
And here are to be answered. Tell me, my daughters
(Since now we will divest us both of rule,
Interest of territory, cares of state),   50
Which of you shall we say doth love us most,
That we our largest bounty may extend
Where nature doth with merit challenge. Goneril,
Our eldest-born, speak first.
Goneril. Sir, I love you more than word can wield the
    matter;   55
Dearer than eyesight, space, and liberty;
Beyond what can be valuèd, rich or rare;
No less than life, with grace, health, beauty, honor;
As much as child e'er loved, or father found;
A love that makes breath poor, and speech unable.   60
Beyond all manner of so much I love you.
Cordelia. [aside] What shall Cordelia speak? Love, and be
    silent.
Lear. Of all these bounds, even from this line to this,
With shadowy forests and with champains riched,
With plenteous rivers and wide-skirted meads,   65
We make thee lady. To thine and Albany's issues
Be this perpetual. — What says our second daughter,
Our dearest Regan, wife of Cornwall?

44 *several* individual   47 *amorous sojourn* i.e. visit of courtship   50 *Interest*
legal possession   53 *nature . . . challenge* natural affection matches other
merits   55 *wield* handle   56 *space* scope (for the exercise of 'liberty')
60 *breath* voice   *unable* inadequate   64 *champains riched* plains enriched
65 *wide-skirted* far-spreading   66 *issues* descendants   67 *perpetual* in perpe-
tuity

 Regan. I am made of that self mettle as my sister,
70 And prize me at her worth. In my true heart
  I find she names my very deed of love;
  Only she comes too short, that I profess
  Myself an enemy to all other joys
  Which the most precious square of sense possesses,
75 And find I am alone felicitate
  In your dear Highness' love.
 Cordelia.   *[aside]* Then poor Cordelia;
  And yet not so, since I am sure my love's
  More ponderous than my tongue.
 Lear. To thee and thine hereditary ever
80 Remain this ample third of our fair kingdom,
  No less in space, validity, and pleasure
  Than that conferred on Goneril. — Now, our joy,
  Although our last and least; to whose young love
  The vines of France and milk of Burgundy
85 Strive to be interest; what can you say to draw
  A third more opulent than your sisters? Speak.
 Cordelia. Nothing, my lord.
 Lear. Nothing?
 Cordelia. Nothing.
90 *Lear.* Nothing will come of nothing. Speak again.
 Cordelia. Unhappy that I am, I cannot heave
  My heart into my mouth. I love your Majesty
  According to my bond, no more nor less.
 Lear. How, how, Cordelia? Mend your speech a little,
  Lest you may mar your fortunes.

---

70 *prize . . . worth* value me at her value 71 *my very deed of* the true fact
of my 74 *Which . . . possesses* which the most precise measurement by the
senses holds to be most precious 75 *felicitate* made happy 78 *ponderous*
weighty 81 *validity* value *pleasure* pleasing qualities 83 *least* smallest,
youngest 84 *vines* vineyards *milk* pasture-lands (?) 85 *interest* concerned
as interested parties 93 *bond* obligation

Cordelia.   Good my lord,   95
 You have begot me, bred me, loved me. I
 Return those duties back as are right fit,
 Obey you, love you, and most honor you.
 Why have my sisters husbands if they say
 They love you all? Haply, when I shall wed,   100
 That lord whose hand must take my plight shall carry
 Half my love with him, half my care and duty.
 Sure I shall never marry like my sisters,
 [To love my father all.]
Lear. But goes thy heart with this?
Cordelia.   Ay, my good lord.   105
Lear. So young, and so untender?
Cordelia. So young, my lord, and true.
Lear. Let it be so, thy truth then be thy dower!
 For, by the sacred radiance of the sun,
 The mysteries of Hecate and the night,   110
 By all the operation of the orbs
 From whom we do exist and cease to be,
 Here I disclaim all my paternal care,
 Propinquity and property of blood,
 And as a stranger to my heart and me   115
 Hold thee from this for ever. The barbarous Scythian,
 Or he that makes his generation messes
 To gorge his appetite, shall to my bosom
 Be as well neighbored, pitied, and relieved,
 As thou my sometime daughter.
Kent.   Good my liege —   120

97 *Return . . . fit* i.e. am fittingly dutiful in return 101 *plight* pledge, troth-plight 110 *Hecate* infernal goddess, patroness of witches 111 *operation . . . orbs* astrological influences 114 *Propinquity* relationship *property* i.e. common property, something shared 116 *Scythian* (proverbially barbarous) 117 *makes . . . messes* makes meals of his offspring 120 *sometime* former

Lear. Peace, Kent!
    Come not between the dragon and his wrath.
    I loved her most, and thought to set my rest
    On her kind nursery. — Hence and avoid my sight! —
125   So be my grave my peace as here I give
    Her father's heart from her! Call France. Who stirs!
    Call Burgundy. Cornwall and Albany,
    With my two daughters' dowers digest the third;
    Let pride, which she calls plainness, marry her.
130   I do invest you jointly with my power,
    Preeminence, and all the large effects
    That troop with majesty. Ourself, by monthly course,
    With reservation of an hundred knights,
    By you to be sustained, shall our abode
135   Make with you by due turn. Only we shall retain
    The name, and all th' addition to a king. The sway,
    Revenue, execution of the rest,
    Belovèd sons, be yours; which to confirm,
    This coronet part between you.
Kent.   Royal Lear,
140   Whom I have ever honored as my king,
    Loved as my father, as my master followed,
    As my great patron thought on in my prayers —
Lear. The bow is bent and drawn; make from the shaft.
Kent. Let it fall rather, though the fork invade
145   The region of my heart. Be Kent unmannerly
    When Lear is mad. What wouldst thou do, old man?
    Think'st thou that duty shall have dread to speak

122 *his* its　123 *set my rest* (1) risk my stake (a term in the card game primero) (2) rely for my repose　124 *nursery* nursing, care　125 *So . . . peace as* let me rest peacefully in my grave only as　131 *effects* tokens　132 *Ourself* I (royal plural)　136 *th' addition* honors and prerogatives　139 *coronet* (symbol of rule, not necessarily the royal crown)　143 *make* make away　144 *fall* strike *fork* two-pronged head

When power to flattery bows? To plainness honor's
　bound
When majesty falls to folly. Reserve thy state,
And in thy best consideration check   150
This hideous rashness. Answer my life my judgment,
Thy youngest daughter does not love thee least,
Nor are those empty-hearted whose low sounds
Reverb no hollowness.

Lear.　　　　　　　　Kent, on thy life, no more!

Kent. My life I never held but as a pawn   155
　To wage against thine enemies; ne'er fear to lose it,
　Thy safety being motive.

Lear.　　　　　　　　Out of my sight!

Kent. See better, Lear, and let me still remain
　The true blank of thine eye.

Lear. Now by Apollo —

Kent.　　　　　　　Now by Apollo, King,   160
　Thou swear'st thy gods in vain.

Lear.　　　　　　　　　　O vassal! Miscreant!
　　　　　　　　　　　　　　[Grasping his sword.]

Albany, Cornwall. Dear sir, forbear!

Kent. Kill thy physician, and thy fee bestow
　Upon the foul disease. Revoke thy gift,
　Or, whilst I can vent clamor from my throat,   165
　I'll tell thee thou dost evil.

Lear.　　　　　　　　Hear me, recreant,
　On thine allegiance, hear me!

---

149 *Reserve thy state* retain your kingly authority 150 *best consideration*
most careful deliberation 151 *Answer my life* i.e. I'll stake my life on
154 *Reverb no hollowness* i.e. do not reverberate (like a drum) as a result
of hollowness 155 *pawn* stake 156 *wage* wager, pit 157 *motive* the
moving cause 158 *still* always 159 blank center of the target (to guide
your aim truly) 161 *Miscreant* (1) rascal (2) infidel 166 *recreant* traitor

That thou hast sought to make us break our vows,
Which we durst never yet, and with strained pride
170   To come betwixt our sentence and our power,
Which nor our nature nor our place can bear,
Our potency made good, take thy reward.
Five days we do allot thee for provision
To shield thee from disasters of the world,
175   And on the sixth to turn thy hated back
Upon our kingdom. If, on the tenth day following,
Thy banished trunk be found in our dominions,
The moment is thy death. Away. By Jupiter,
This shall not be revoked.

180 *Kent.* Fare thee well, King. Sith thus thou wilt appear,
Freedom lives hence, and banishment is here.
[To Cordelia] The gods to their dear shelter take thee, maid,
That justly think'st and hast most rightly said.
[To Regan and Goneril] And your large speeches may your
   deeds approve,
185   That good effects may spring from words of love.
Thus Kent, O princes, bids you all adieu;
He'll shape his old course in a country new.   *Exit.*

Flourish. Enter Gloucester, with France and Burgundy;
   Attendants.

Gloucester. Here's France and Burgundy, my noble lord.
Lear. My Lord of Burgundy,
190   We first address toward you, who with this king
Hath rivalled for our daughter. What in the least

168 *That* in that, since 169 *strained* excessive 170 *To come ... power* i.e.
to oppose my power to sentence 172 *Our ... good* if my power is to be
demonstrated as real 174 *disasters* accidents 177 *trunk* body 180 *Sith*
since 184 *approve* confirm 185 *effects* consequences 187 *shape ... course*
keep to his customary ways (of honesty)

Will you require in present dower with her,
Or cease your quest of love?
Burgundy.   Most royal Majesty,
I crave no more than hath your Highness offered,
Nor will you tender less.
Lear.   Right noble Burgundy,   195
When she was dear to us, we did hold her so;
But now her price is fallen. Sir, there she stands.
If aught within that little seeming substance,
Or all of it, with our displeasure pieced
And nothing more, may fitly like your Grace,   200
She's there, and she is yours.
Burgundy.   I know no answer.
Lear. Will you, with those infirmities she owes,
Unfriended, new adopted to our hate,
Dow'red with our curse, and strangered with our oath,
Take her, or leave her?
Burgundy.   Pardon me, royal sir.   205
Election makes not up on such conditions.
Lear. Then leave her, sir, for by the pow'r that made me
I tell you all her wealth. *[to France]* For you, great King,
I would not from your love make such a stray
To match you where I hate; therefore beseech you   210
T' avert your liking a more worthier way
Than on a wretch whom nature is ashamed
Almost t' acknowledge hers.
France.   This is most strange,
That she whom even but now was your best object,
The argument of your praise, balm of your age,   215

198 *seeming substance* i.e. nothing, mere shell 199 *pieced* joined 202 *owes* owns 204 *strangered with* made alien by 206 *Election . . . conditions* no choice is possible on such terms 209 *make . . . stray* stray so far as 211 *avert* turn 214 *best* favorite 215 *argument* theme

The best, the dearest, should in this trice of time
Commit a thing so monstrous to dismantle
So many folds of favor. Sure her offense
Must be of such unnatural degree
220   That monsters it, or your fore-vouched affection
Fall'n into taint; which to believe of her
Must be a faith that reason without miracle
Should never plant in me.
   Cordelia.   I yet beseech your Majesty,
If for I want that glib and oily art
225   To speak and purpose not since what I well intend
I'll do't before I speak, that you make known
It is no vicious blot, murder, or foulness,
No unchaste action or dishonorèd step,
That hath deprived me of your grace and favor;
230   But even for want of that for which I am richer —
A still-soliciting eye, and such a tongue
That I am glad I have not, though not to have it
Hath lost me in your liking.
   Lear.   Better thou
Hadst not been born than not t' have pleased me better.
235 *France.* Is it but this? A tardiness in nature
Which often leaves the history unspoke
That it intends to do. My Lord of Burgundy,
What say you to the lady? Love's not love

217 *to dismantle* so to strip off   220 *That monsters it* as makes it monstrous
(i.e. abnormal, freakish) *fore-vouched* previously sworn   221 *taint* decay
(with the implication that the affection, and the oath attesting it, were
tainted in the first place)   222 *reason . . . miracle* i.e. rational, unaided by
miraculous, means of persuasion   225 *purpose not* i.e. without intending
to act in accordance with my words   231 *still-soliciting* always-begging
235 *tardiness in nature* natural reticence   236 *history unspoke* actions unan-
nounced

When it is mingled with regards that stands
Aloof from th' entire point. Will you have her?   240
She is herself a dowry.
Burgundy.   Royal King,
Give but that portion which yourself proposed,
And here I take Cordelia by the hand,
Duchess of Burgundy.
Lear. Nothing. I have sworn. I am firm.   245
Burgundy. I am sorry then you have so lost a father
That you must lose a husband.
Cordelia.   Peace be with Burgundy.
Since that respects of fortune are his love,
I shall not be his wife.
France. Fairest Cordelia, that art most rich being poor,   250
Most choice forsaken, and most loved despised,
Thee and thy virtues here I seize upon.
Be it lawful I take up what's cast away.
Gods, gods! 'Tis strange that from their cold'st neglect
My love should kindle to inflamed respect.   255
Thy dow'rless daughter, King, thrown to my chance,
Is queen of us, of ours, and our fair France.
Not all the dukes of wat'rish Burgundy
Can buy this unprized precious maid of me.
Bid them farewell, Cordelia, though unkind.   260
Thou losest here, a better where to find.
Lear. Thou hast her, France; let her be thine, for we
Have no such daughter, nor shall ever see
That face of hers again. Therefore be gone

239–40 *mingled . . . point* i.e. mixed with irrelevant considerations 248 *re-spects* considerations 255 *inflamed respect* ardent regard 258 *wat'rish* (1) watery, weak (2) watered, diluted 259 *unprized* unvalued 261 *here* this place *where* other place

265   Without our grace, our love, our benison.
       Come, noble Burgundy.
          Flourish. Exeunt [Lear, Burgundy, Cornwall, Albany,
                         Gloucester, and Attendants].
       France. Bid farewell to your sisters.
       Cordelia. The jewels of our father, with washed eyes
       Cordelia leaves you. I know you what you are;
270   And, like a sister, am most loath to call
       Your faults as they are named. Love well our father.
       To your professèd bosoms I commit him;
       But yet, alas, stood I within his grace,
       I would prefer him to a better place.
275   So farewell to you both.
       Regan. Prescribe not us our duty.
       Goneril.   Let your study
       Be to content your lord, who hath received you
       At fortune's alms. You have obedience scanted,
       And well are worth the want that you have wanted.
       Cordelia. Time shall unfold what plighted cunning
280   hides,
       Who covers faults, at last with shame derides.
       Well may you prosper.
       France.   Come, my fair Cordelia.
                   Exit France and Cordelia.
       Goneril. Sister, it is not little I have to say of what most
       nearly appertains to us both. I think our father will hence
285   to-night.

---

265 *benison* blessing   268 *jewels* i.e. things held precious (cf. l. 259) *washed* tear-washed   270 *like a sister* i.e. with sisterly loyalty   271 *as . . . named* by their true names   272 *professèd* i.e. love-professing   274 *prefer* promote 278 *alms* small offerings   279 *worth . . . wanted* i.e. deserving no affection since you have shown no affection   280 *plighted* pleated, enfolded   281 *Who . . . derides* i.e. time at first conceals faults, then exposes them to shame

Regan. That's most certain, and with you; next month with
   us.

Goneril. You see how full of changes his age is. The ob-
   servation we have made of it hath not been little. He always loved our sister most, and with what poor judgment   290
   he hath now cast her off appears too grossly.

Regan. 'Tis the infirmity of his age; yet he hath ever but
   slenderly known himself.

Goneril. The best and soundest of his time hath been but
   rash; then must we look from his age to receive not alone   295
   the imperfections of long-ingraffed condition, but therewithal the unruly waywardness that infirm and choleric
   years bring with them.

Regan. Such unconstant starts are we like to have from him
   as this of Kent's banishment.   300

Goneril. There is further compliment of leave-taking between France and him. Pray you let us hit together; if
   our father carry authority with such disposition as he
   bears, this last surrender of his will but offend us.

Regan. We shall further think of it.   305

Goneril. We must do something, and i' th' heat.   *Exeunt.*

Enter Bastard [Edmund, solus, with a letter].   I, ii

Edmund. Thou, Nature, art my goddess; to thy law
   My services are bound. Wherefore should I

291 *grossly* crudely conspicuous   293 *known himself* i.e. been aware of
what he truly is   294 *of his time* period of his past life   296 *long-ingraffed*
ingrown, chronic   296–97 *therewithal* along with that   299 *unconstant
starts* impulsive moves   301 *compliment* formality   302 *hit* agree   304 *surrender* i.e. yielding up of authority   *offend* harm   306 *i' th' heat* i.e. while
the iron is hot   I, ii, 1 *Nature* i.e. the material and mechanistic as distinct
from the spiritual and heaven-ordained

Stand in the plague of custom, and permit
The curiosity of nations to deprive me,
5 For that I am some twelve or fourteen moonshines
Lag of a brother? Why bastard? Wherefore base,
When my dimensions are as well compact,
My mind as generous, and my shape as true,
As honest madam's issue? Why brand they us
10 With base? with baseness? Bastardy base? Base?
Who, in the lusty stealth of nature, take
More composition and fierce quality
Than doth, within a dull, stale, tirèd bed,
Go to th' creating a whole tribe of fops
15 Got 'tween asleep and wake? Well then,
Legitimate Edgar, I must have your land.
Our father's love is to the bastard Edmund
As to th' legitimate. Fine word, 'legitimate.'
Well, my legitimate, if this letter speed,
20 And my invention thrive, Edmund the base
Shall top th' legitimate. I grow, I prosper.
Now, gods, stand up for bastards.

Enter Gloucester.

Gloucester. Kent banished thus? and France in choler parted?
And the King gone to-night? prescribed his pow'r?
25 Confined to exhibition? All this done
Upon the gad? Edmund, how now? What news?

3 *Stand . . . custom* submit to the affliction of convention 4 *curiosity* nice
distinctions 5 *For that* because *moonshines* months 6 *Lag of* behind (in
age) 7 *compact* fitted, matched 8 *generous* befitting the high-born
9 *honest* chaste 11 *lusty . . . nature* secrecy of natural lust 12 *composition*
completeness of constitution, robustness *fierce* mettlesome, thoroughbred
14 *fops* fools 15 *Got* begotten 20 *invention thrive* plot succeed 24 *prescribed* limited 25 *exhibition* an allowance, a pension 26 *gad* spur

46

Edmund. So please your lordship, none.

Gloucester. Why so earnestly seek you to put up that letter?

Edmund. I know no news, my lord.

Gloucester. What paper were you reading?   30

Edmund. Nothing, my lord.

Gloucester. No? What needed then that terrible dispatch of
it into your pocket? The quality of nothing hath not such
need to hide itself. Let's see. Come, if it be nothing, I shall
not need spectacles.   35

Edmund. I beseech you, sir, pardon me. It is a letter from
my brother that I have not all o'er-read; and for so much
as I have perused, I find it not fit for your o'erlooking.

Gloucester. Give me the letter, sir.

Edmund. I shall offend, either to detain or give it. The con- 40
tents, as in part I understand them, are to blame.

Gloucester. Let's see, let's see.

Edmund. I hope, for my brother's justification, he wrote
this but as an essay or taste of my virtue.

Gloucester. (*reads*) 'This policy and reverence of age makes 45
the world bitter to the best of our times; keeps our fortunes from us till our oldness cannot relish them. I begin
to find an idle and fond bondage in the oppression of aged
tyranny, who sways, not as it hath power, but as it is suffered. Come to me, that of this I may speak more. If our   50
father would sleep till I waked him, you should enjoy half
his revenue for ever, and live the beloved of your brother,
                                                    EDGAR.'

Hum! Conspiracy? 'Sleep till I waked him, you should
enjoy half his revenue.' My son Edgar! Had he a hand to 55

28 *put up* put away   38 *o'erlooking* examination   41 *to blame* blameworthy
44 *essay* trial   *taste* test   45 *policy and reverence* policy of reverencing
46 *the best of our times* our best years   48 *idle, fond* foolish (synonyms)
49 *who sways* which rules   49–50 *suffered* allowed   52 *revenue* income

write this? A heart and brain to breed it in? When came
you to this? Who brought it?

Edmund. It was not brought me, my lord; there's the cunning of it. I found it thrown in at the casement of my
60 closet.

Gloucester. You know the character to be your brother's?

Edmund. If the matter were good, my lord, I durst swear it
were his; but in respect of that, I would fain think it were
not.

65 *Gloucester.* It is his.

Edmund. It is his hand, my lord; but I hope his heart is not
in the contents.

Gloucester. Has he never before sounded you in this business?

70 *Edmund.* Never, my lord. But I have heard him oft maintain it to be fit that, sons at perfect age, and fathers declined, the father should be as ward to the son, and the son
manage his revenue.

Gloucester. O villain, villain! His very opinion in the letter.
75 Abhorred villain, unnatural, detested, brutish villain;
worse than brutish! Go, sirrah, seek him. I'll apprehend
him. Abominable villain! Where is he?

Edmund. I do not well know, my lord. If it shall please you
to·suspend your indignation against my brother till you
80 can derive from him better testimony of his intent, you
should run a certain course; where, if you violently proceed against him, mistaking his purpose, it would make a
great gap in your own honor and shake in pieces the
heart of his obedience. I dare pawn down my life for him

57 *to this* upon this   59 *casement* window   60 *closet* room   61 *character*
handwriting   62 *matter* contents   63 *in respect of that* i.e. considering
what those contents are   *fain* prefer to   68 *sounded you* sounded you out
71 *perfect age* prime of life   76 *sirrah* sir (familiar, or contemptuous,
form)   81 *run . . . course* i.e. know where you are going

that he hath writ this to feel my affection to your honor, 85
and to no other pretense of danger.

Gloucester. Think you so?

Edmund. If your honor judge it meet, I will place you where
you shall hear us confer of this and by an auricular assurance have your satisfaction, and that without any further 90
delay than this very evening.

Gloucester. He cannot be such a monster.

[*Edmund.* Nor is not, sure.

Gloucester. To his father, that so tenderly and entirely loves
him. Heaven and earth!] Edmund, seek him out; wind 95
me into him, I pray you; frame the business after your
own wisdom. I would unstate myself to be in a due resolution.

Edmund. I will seek him, sir, presently; convey the business
as I shall find means, and acquaint you withal. 100

Gloucester. These late eclipses in the sun and moon portend
no good to us. Though the wisdom of nature can reason
it thus and thus, yet nature finds itself scourged by the
sequent effects. Love cools, friendship falls off, brothers
divide. In cities, mutinies; in countries, discord; in pal- 105
aces, treason; and the bond cracked 'twixt son and father.
This villain of mine comes under the prediction, there's
son against father; the King falls from bias of nature,
there's father against child. We have seen the best of our

85 *feel* feel out, test *affection* attachment, loyalty 86 *pretense of danger*
dangerous intention 88 *judge it meet* consider it fitting 89–90 *by . . .
assurance* i.e. by the proof of your own ears 95–96 *wind me* worm 96
frame plan 97–98 *unstate . . . resolution* i.e. give everything to know for
certain 99 *presently* at once *convey* conduct 100 *withal* therewith 101
late recent 102 *wisdom of nature* natural lore, science 102–4 *can . . . effects*
i.e. can supply explanations, yet punitive upheavals in nature (such as
earthquakes) follow 103 *scourged* whipped 104 *sequent* following
105 *mutinies* rebellions 107 *comes . . . prediction* i.e. is included among
these ill-omened things 108 *bias of nature* natural tendency

49

110 time. Machinations, hollowness, treachery, and all ruinous
disorders follow us disquietly to our graves. Find out this
villain, Edmund, it shall lose thee nothing; do it carefully. And the noble and true-hearted Kent banished; his
offense, honesty. 'Tis strange.   *Exit.*

115 *Edmund.* This is the excellent foppery of the world, that
when we are sick in fortune, often the surfeits of our own
behavior, we make guilty of our disasters the sun, the
moon, and stars; as if we were villains on necessity; fools
by heavenly compulsion; knaves, thieves, and treachers
120 by spherical predominance; drunkards, liars, and adul-
terers by an enforced obedience of planetary influence;
and all that we are evil in, by a divine thrusting on. An
admirable evasion of whoremaster man, to lay his goatish
disposition on the charge of a star. My father compounded
125 with my mother under the Dragon's Tail, and my na-
tivity was under Ursa Major, so that it follows I am rough
and lecherous. Fut! I should have been that I am, had the
maidenliest star in the firmament twinkled on my bastardizing. Edgar —

Enter Edgar.

130 and pat he comes, like the catastrophe of the old comedy.
My cue is villainous melancholy, with a sigh like Tom o'
Bedlam. — O, these eclipses do portend these divisions.
Fa, sol, la, mi.

112 *lose thee nothing* i.e. you will not lose by it   115 *foppery* foolishness
116 *we are sick . . . surfeits* i.e. our fortunes grow sickly, often from the
excesses   119 *treachers* traitors   120 *spherical predominance* i.e. ascendancy,
or rule, of a particular sphere   123 *goatish* lecherous   124 *compounded*
(1) came to terms (2) created   125, 126 *Dragon's Tail, Ursa Major* (con-
stellations, cited because of the suggestiveness of their names)   125–26 *na-
tivity* birthday   130 *catastrophe* conclusion   131–32 *Tom o' Bedlam* (a type
of beggar, mad or pretending to be, so named from the London madhouse,
Bethlehem or 'Bedlam' Hospital)

Edgar. How now, brother Edmund; what serious contem-   135
plation are you in?

Edmund. I am thinking, brother, of a prediction I read this
other day, what should follow these eclipses.

Edgar. Do you busy yourself with that?

Edmund. I promise you, the effects he writes of succeed unhappily: [as of unnaturalness between the child and the   140
parent; death, dearth, dissolutions of ancient amities; divisions in state, menaces and maledictions against king
and nobles; needless diffidences, banishment of friends,
dissipation of cohorts, nuptial breaches, and I know not
what.   145

Edgar. How long have you been a sectary astronomical?

Edmund. Come, come,] when saw you my father last?

Edgar. The night gone by.

Edmund. Spake you with him?

Edgar. Ay, two hours together.   150

Edmund. Parted you in good terms? Found you no displeasure in him by word nor countenance?

Edgar. None at all.

Edmund. Bethink yourself wherein you may have offended
him; and at my entreaty forbear his presence until some   155
little time hath qualified the heat of his displeasure, which
at this instant so rageth in him that with the mischief of
your person it would scarcely allay.

Edgar. Some villain hath done me wrong.

Edmund. That's my fear. I pray you have a continent for-   160
bearance till the speed of his rage goes slower; and, as I

139-40 *succeed unhappily* unluckily follow   140 *unnaturalness* unkindness,
enmity   143 *diffidences* instances of distrust   144 *dissipation of cohorts*
melting away of supporters   146 *sectary astronomical* of the astrological
sect   152 *countenance* expression, look   156 *qualified* moderated   157 *mischief* injury   158 *allay* be appeased   160-61 *continent forbearance* cautious
inaccessibility

51

say, retire with me to my lodging, from whence I will
fitly bring you to hear my lord speak. Pray ye, go;
there's my key. If you do stir abroad, go armed.

165 *Edgar.* Armed, brother?

Edmund. Brother, I advise you to the best. Go armed. I am
no honest man if there be any good meaning toward you.
I have told you what I have seen and heard; but faintly,
nothing like the image and horror of it. Pray you, away.

170 *Edgar.* Shall I hear from you anon?

Edmund. I do serve you in this business.   *Exit [Edgar].*
A credulous father, and a brother noble,
Whose nature is so far from doing harms
That he suspects none; on whose foolish honesty

175 My practices ride easy. I see the business.
Let me, if not by birth, have lands by wit;
All with me's meet that I can fashion fit.   *Exit.*

I, iii   *Enter Goneril and Steward [Oswald].*

Goneril. Did my father strike my gentleman for chiding of
his fool?

Oswald. Ay, madam.

Goneril. By day and night, he wrongs me! Every hour
He flashes into one gross crime or other

5 That sets us all at odds. I'll not endure it.
His knights grow riotous, and himself upbraids us
On every trifle. When he returns from hunting,
I will not speak with him. Say I am sick.

---

163 *fitly* conveniently 169 *image and horror* horrible true picture 170 *anon*
soon 175 *practices* plots 176 *wit* intelligence 177 *meet* proper, acceptable
fashion fit i.e. rig up, shape to the purpose I, iii, 3 *day and night* (an oath)
4 *crime* offense 6 *riotous* boisterous

If you come slack of former services,
You shall do well; the fault of it I'll answer.   10
                                    [Horns within.]
Oswald. He's coming, madam; I hear him.
Goneril. Put on what weary negligence you please,
    You and your fellows. I'd have it come to question.
    If he distaste it, let him to my sister,
    Whose mind and mine I know in that are one,   15
    [Not to be overruled. Idle old man,
    That still would manage those authorities
    That he hath given away. Now, by my life,
    Old fools are babes again, and must be used
    With checks as flatteries, when they are seen abused.] 20
    Remember what I have said.
Oswald.   Well, madam.
Goneril. And let his knights have colder looks among you.
    What grows of it, no matter; advise your fellows so.
    [I would breed from hence occasions, and I shall,
    That I may speak.] I'll write straight to my sister   25
    To hold my course. Prepare for dinner.   *Exeunt.*

                Enter Kent [disguised].   I, iv

Kent. If but as well I other accents borrow
    That can my speech defuse, my good intent
    May carry through itself to that full issue
    For which I razed my likeness. Now, banished Kent,
    If thou canst serve where thou dost stand condemned,   5

9 *come . . . services* i.e. serve him less well than formerly   10 *answer* answer
for   13 *question* i.e. open issue, a thing discussed   14 *distaste* dislike
16 *Idle* foolish   20 *checks . . . abused* restraints in place of cajolery when
they (the old men) are seen to be deceived (about their true state)   24-25
breed . . . speak i.e. make an issue of it so that I may speak   I, iv, 2 *defuse*
disorder, disguise   3 *full issue* perfect result   4 *razed my likeness* erased
my natural appearance

So may it come, thy master whom thou lov'st
Shall find thee full of labors.

Horns within. Enter Lear, [Knight,] and Attendants.

Lear. Let me not stay a jot for dinner; go get it ready. *[Exit
an Attendant.]* How now, what art thou?

10 *Kent.* A man, sir.

Lear. What dost thou profess? What wouldst thou with us?

Kent. I do profess to be no less than I seem, to serve him
truly that will put me in trust, to love him that is honest,
to converse with him that is wise and says little, to fear

15   judgment, to fight when I cannot choose, and to eat no
fish.

Lear. What art thou?

Kent. A very honest-hearted fellow, and as poor as the
King.

20 *Lear.* If thou be'st as poor for a subject as he's for a king,
thou art poor enough. What wouldst thou?

Kent. Service.

Lear. Who wouldst thou serve?

Kent. You.

25 *Lear.* Dost thou know me, fellow?

Kent. No, sir, but you have that in your countenance which
I would fain call master.

Lear. What's that?

Kent. Authority.

30 *Lear.* What services canst thou do?

Kent. I can keep honest counsel, ride, run, mar a curious
tale in telling it and deliver a plain message bluntly. That

8 *stay* wait   11 *profess* do, work at (with pun following)   12 *profess.*
claim   14 *converse* associate   15 *judgment* i.e. God's judgment   15–16 *eat
no fish* be a Protestant (anachronism), or avoid unmanly diet (?)   27 *fain*
like to   31 *keep honest counsel* keep counsel honestly, i.e. respect confidences
curious elaborate, embroidered (as contrasted with 'plain')

which ordinary men are fit for I am qualified in, and the
best of me is diligence.

Lear. How old art thou?   35

Kent. Not so young, sir, to love a woman for singing, nor
so old to dote on her for anything. I have years on my
back forty-eight.

Lear. Follow me; thou shalt serve me. If I like thee no
worse after dinner, I will not part from thee yet. Dinner, 40
ho, dinner! Where's my knave? my fool? Go you and
call my fool hither.   *[Exit an Attendant.]*

Enter Steward [Oswald].

You, you, sirrah, where's my daughter?

Oswald. So please you ——   *Exit.*

Lear. What says the fellow there? Call the clotpoll back. 45
[Exit Knight.] Where's my fool? Ho, I think the world's
asleep.

[Enter Knight.]

How now? Where's that mongrel?

Knight. He says, my lord, your daughter is not well.

Lear. Why came not the slave back to me when I called 50
him?

Knight. Sir, he answered me in the roundest manner, he
would not.

Lear. He would not?

Knight. My lord, I know not what the matter is; but to my 55
judgment your Highness is not entertained with that cere-
monious affection as you were wont. There's a great
abatement of kindness appears as well in the general dependants as in the Duke himself also and your daughter.

41 *knave* boy   45 *clotpoll* clodpoll, dolt   56 *entertained* rendered hospi-
tality

60 *Lear.* Ha? Say'st thou so?

    Knight. I beseech you pardon me, my lord, if I be mistaken; for my duty cannot be silent when I think your Highness wronged.

    Lear. Thou but rememb'rest me of mine own conception.
65 I have perceived a most faint neglect of late, which I have rather blamed as mine own jealous curiosity than as a very pretense and purpose of unkindness. I will look further into't. But where's my fool? I have not seen him this two days.

70 *Knight.* Since my young lady's going into France, sir, the fool hath much pined away.

    Lear. No more of that; I have noted it well. Go you and tell my daughter I would speak with her. *[Exit Knight.]* Go you, call hither my fool.   *[Exit an Attendant.]*

Enter Steward [Oswald].

75 O, you, sir, you! Come you hither, sir. Who am I, sir?

    Oswald. My lady's father.

    Lear. 'My lady's father'? My lord's knave, you whoreson dog, you slave, you cur!

    Oswald. I am none of these, my lord; I beseech your pardon.
80 *Lear.* Do you bandy looks with me, you rascal?

                             [Strikes him.]

    Oswald. I'll not be strucken, my lord.

    Kent. Nor tripped neither, you base football player.

                            [Trips up his heels.]

    Lear. I thank thee, fellow. Thou serv'st me, and I'll love thee.

---

64 *rememb'rest* remind   65 *faint neglect* i.e. the 'weary negligence' of I, iii, 12   66 *jealous curiosity* i.e. suspicious concern about trifles   66–67 *very pretense* true intention   80 *bandy* volley, exchange   81 *strucken* struck 82 *football* (an impromptu street and field game, held in low esteem)

Kent. Come, sir, arise, away. I'll teach you differences. 85
Away, away. If you will measure your lubber's length
again, tarry; but away. Go to! Have you wisdom? So.
                                        [Pushes him out.]
Lear. Now, my friendly knave, I thank thee. There's earnest of thy service.   *[Gives money.]*

Enter Fool.

Fool. Let me hire him too. Here's my coxcomb.   90
                                        [Offers Kent his cap.]
Lear. How now, my pretty knave? How dost thou?
Fool. Sirrah, you were best take my coxcomb.
Kent. Why, fool?
Fool. Why? For taking one's part that's out of favor. Nay,
an thou canst not smile as the wind sits, thou'lt catch cold 95
shortly. There, take my coxcomb. Why, this fellow has
banished two on's daughters, and did the third a blessing
against his will. If thou follow him, thou must needs wear
my coxcomb. —How now, nuncle? Would I had two
coxcombs and two daughters.   100
Lear. Why, my boy?
Fool. If I gave them all my living, I'ld keep my coxcombs
myself. There's mine; beg another of thy daughters.
Lear. Take heed, sirrah—the whip.
Fool. Truth's a dog must to kennel; he must be whipped 105
out, when the Lady Brach may stand by th' fire and
stink.
Lear. A pestilent gall to me.

85 *differences* distinctions in rank   87 *Go to! . . . wisdom* i.e. Get along!
Do you know what's good for you?   88–89 *earnest* part payment   90 *coxcomb* (cap of the professional fool, topped with an imitation comb)
95 *smile . . . sits* i.e. adapt yourself to prevailing forces   97 *banished* i.e.
provided the means for them to become alien to him   99 *nuncle* mine
uncle   106 *Brach* hound bitch   108 *gall* sore, source of irritation

    Fool. Sirrah, I'll teach thee a speech.
110 *Lear.* Do.
    Fool. Mark it, nuncle.

            Have more than thou showest,
            Speak less than thou knowest,
            Lend less than thou owest,
115   Ride more than thou goest,
            Learn more than thou trowest,
            Set less than thou throwest;
            Leave thy drink and thy whore,
            And keep in-a-door,
120   And thou shalt have more
            Than two tens to a score.

    Kent. This is nothing, fool.
    Fool. Then 'tis like the breath of an unfee'd lawyer – you
gave me nothing for't. Can you make no use of nothing,
125 nuncle?
    Lear. Why, no, boy. Nothing can be made out of nothing.
    Fool. [to Kent] Prithee tell him, so much the rent of his land
comes to; he will not believe a fool.
    Lear. A bitter fool.
130 *Fool.* Dost thou know the difference, my boy, between a
bitter fool and a sweet one?
    Lear. No, lad; teach me.
    Fool.   [That lord that counselled thee
            To give away thy land,
135   Come place him here by me –
            Do thou for him stand.

114 *owest* borrow (?) own, keep (?)   115 *goest* walk   116 *Learn* hear, listen to *trowest* believe   117 *Set . . . throwest* stake less than you throw for
(i.e. play for odds)   120–21 *have . . . score* i.e. do better than break even
123 *breath* voice, counsel (reliable only when paid for)   127 *rent . . . land*
(nothing, since he has no land)   131 *bitter, sweet* satirical, non-satirical
136 *Do . . . stand* (the Fool thus identifying Lear as his own foolish counsellor)

The sweet and bitter fool
　　Will presently appear;
　　The one in motley here,
　　　The other found out there.   140

Lear. Dost thou call me fool, boy?

Fool. All thy other titles thou hast given away; that thou
　　was born with.

Kent. This is not altogether fool, my lord.

Fool. No, faith; lords and great men will not let me. If I   145
　　had a monopoly out, they would have part on't. And
　　ladies too, they will not let me have all the fool to myself;
　　they'll be snatching.] Nuncle, give me an egg, and I'll
　　give thee two crowns.

Lear. What two crowns shall they be?   150

Fool. Why, after I have cut the egg i' th' middle and eat up
　　the meat, the two crowns of the egg. When thou clovest
　　thy crown i' th' middle and gav'st away both parts, thou
　　bor'st thine ass on thy back o'er the dirt. Thou hadst
　　little wit in thy bald crown when thou gav'st thy golden   155
　　one away. If I speak like myself in this, let him be whipped
　　that first finds it so.

　　[Sings] Fools had ne'er less grace in a year,
　　　　For wise men are grown foppish,
　　　　And know not how their wits to wear,   160
　　　　Their manners are so apish.

Lear. When were you wont to be so full of songs, sirrah?

---

140 *found out* revealed (since Lear is the 'born' fool as distinct from himself, the fool in motley, professionally satirical)   145 *let me* (i.e. be all fool,
since they seek a share of folly)   148 *snatching* (like greedy courtiers seeking shares in royal patents of monopoly)   154 *bor'st . . . dirt* (thus foolishly
reversing normal behavior)   156 *like myself* i.e. like a fool   156-57 *let . . .
so* i.e. let him be whipped (as a fool) who mistakes this truth as my typical
folly   158 *grace . . . year* favor at any time   159 *foppish* foolish   160 *their
wits to wear* i.e. to use their intelligence

Fool. I have used it, nuncle, e'er since thou mad'st thy
    daughters thy mothers; for when thou gav'st them the
165   rod, and put'st down thine own breeches,
    [Sings] Then they for sudden joy did weep,
          And I for sorrow sung,
        That such a king should play bo-peep
        And go the fools among.
170   Prithee, nuncle, keep a schoolmaster that can teach thy
    fool to lie. I would fain learn to lie.
Lear. An you lie, sirrah, we'll have you whipped.
Fool. I marvel what kin thou and thy daughters are. They'll
    have me whipped for speaking true; thou'lt have me
175   whipped for lying; and sometimes I am whipped for
    holding my peace. I had rather be any kind o' thing than
    a fool, and yet I would not be thee, nuncle: thou hast
    pared thy wit o' both sides and left nothing i' th' middle.
    Here comes one o' the parings.

Enter Goneril.

180 *Lear.* How now, daughter? What makes that frontlet on?
    You are too much of late i' th' frown.
Fool. Thou wast a pretty fellow when thou hadst no need to
    care for her frowning. Now thou art an O without a
    figure. I am better than thou art now: I am a fool, thou
185   art nothing. *[to Goneril]* Yes, forsooth, I will hold my
    tongue. So your face bids me, though you say nothing.
    Mum, mum,

163 *used* practiced   168 *play bo-peep* i.e. act like a child   172 *An* if
178 *pared . . . middle* i.e. completely disposed of your wits (in disposing
of your power)   180 *frontlet* band worn across the brow; hence, frown
183–84 *O . . . figure* cipher without a digit to give it value

He that keeps nor crust nor crum,
Weary of all, shall want some. —
[Points at Lear.] That's a shealed peascod.   190
Goneril. Not only, sir, this your all-licensed fool,
But other of your insolent retinue
Do hourly carp and quarrel, breaking forth
In rank and not-to-be-endurèd riots. Sir,
I had thought by making this well known unto you   195
To have found a safe redress, but now grow fearful,
By what yourself too late have spoke and done,
That you protect this course, and put it on
By your allowance; which if you should, the fault
Would not 'scape censure, nor the redresses sleep,   200
Which, in the tender of a wholesome weal,
Might in their working do you that offense,
Which else were shame, that then necessity
Will call discreet proceeding.
Fool. For you know, nuncle,   205
          The hedge-sparrow fed the cuckoo so long
          That it's had it head bit off by it young.
So out went the candle, and we were left darkling.
Lear. Are you our daughter?
Goneril. I would you would make use of your good wisdom   210
     (Whereof I know you are fraught) and put away

188 *crum* soft bread within the crust   189 *want* need   190 *shealed* shelled,
empty   *peascod* pea-pod   191 *all-licensed* all-privileged   193 *carp* complain
196 *safe* sure   198 *put it on* instigate it   199 *allowance* approval   200 *redresses sleep* correction lie dormant   201 *tender of* care for   *weal* state   202–4
Might . . . proceeding in their operation might be considered humiliating
to you but, under the circumstances, are merely prudent   206 *cuckoo* (an
image suggesting illegitimacy as well as voraciousness, since the cuckoo
lays its eggs in the nests of other birds)   207 *it* its   208 *darkling* in the
dark (like the dead hedge-sparrow and the threatened Lear)   211 *fraught*
freighted, laden

61

These dispositions which of late transport you
From what you rightly are.
Fool. May not an ass know when the cart draws the horse?
215   Whoop, Jug, I love thee!
Lear. Does any here know me? This is not Lear.
Does Lear walk thus? speak thus? Where are his eyes?
Either his notion weakens, his discernings
Are lethargied — Ha! Waking? 'Tis not so.
220   Who is it that can tell me who I am?
Fool. Lear's shadow.
[*Lear.* I would learn that; for, by the marks of sovereignty,
Knowledge, and reason, I should be false persuaded
I had daughters.
225 *Fool.* Which they will make an obedient father.]
Lear. Your name, fair gentlewoman?
Goneril. This admiration, sir, is much o' th' savor
Of other your new pranks. I do beseech you
To understand my purposes aright.
230   As you are old and reverend, should be wise.
Here do you keep a hundred knights and squires,
Men so disordered, so deboshed, and bold
That this our court, infected with their manners,
Shows like a riotous inn. Epicurism and lust
235   Makes it more like a tavern or a brothel
Than a graced palace. The shame itself doth speak
For instant remedy. Be then desired
By her that else will take the thing she begs

212 *dispositions* moods 215 *Jug* Joan (evidently part of some catch-phrase)
218 *notion* understanding 219 *Ha! Waking* i.e. so I am really awake
(presumably accompanied by the 'business' of pinching himself) 222
marks of sovereignty evidences that I am King (and hence the father of the
princesses) 227 *admiration* air of wonderment 232 *deboshed* debauched
234 *Epicurism* loose living 236 *graced* honored *shame* disgrace

A little to disquantity your train,
And the remainders that shall still depend   240
To be such men as may besort your age,
Which know themselves, and you.
Lear.   Darkness and devils!
Saddle my horses; call my train together.
Degenerate bastard, I'll not trouble thee:
Yet have I left a daughter.   245
Goneril. You strike my people, and your disordered rabble
Make servants of their betters.

Enter Albany.

Lear. Woe that too late repents. — [O, sir, are you come?]
Is it your will? Speak, sir. — Prepare my horses.
Ingratitude! thou marble-hearted fiend,   250
More hideous when thou show'st thee in a child
Than the sea-monster.
Albany.   Pray, sir, be patient.
Lear. Detested kite, thou liest.
My train are men of choice and rarest parts,
That all particulars of duty know   255
And in the most exact regard support
The worships of their name. O most small fault,
How ugly didst thou in Cordelia show!
Which, like an engine, wrenched my frame of nature
From the fixed place; drew from my heart all love   260

239 *disquantity your train* reduce the size of your retinue 240 *depend* be
attached 241 *besort* befit 242 *Which know* i.e. who are aware of the status
of 244 *Degenerate* unnatural, fallen away from kind 253 *Detested kite*
detestable bird of prey 254 *parts* accomplishments 256 *exact regard*
careful attention, punctiliousness 257 *worships* honor 259 *engine* destruc-
tive contrivance of war 259–60 *wrenched . . . place* set askew my natural
structure, distorted my normal self

And added to the gall. O Lear, Lear, Lear!
Beat at this gate that let thy folly in   *[Strikes his head.]*
And thy dear judgment out. Go, go, my people.
Albany. My lord, I am guiltless, as I am ignorant
Of what hath moved you.
265 *Lear.*   It may be so, my lord.
Hear, Nature, hear; dear goddess, hear:
Suspend thy purpose if thou didst intend
To make this creature fruitful.
Into her womb convey sterility,
270 Dry up in her the organs of increase,
And from her derogate body never spring
A babe to honor her. If she must teem,
Create her child of spleen, that it may live
And be a thwart disnatured torment to her.
275 Let it stamp wrinkles in her brow of youth,
With cadent tears fret channels in her cheeks,
Turn all her mother's pains and benefits
To laughter and contempt, that she may feel
How sharper than a serpent's tooth it is
280 To have a thankless child. Away, away!   *Exit.*
Albany. Now, gods that we adore, whereof comes this?
Goneril. Never afflict yourself to know more of it,
But let his disposition have that scope
As dotage gives it.

Enter Lear.

285 *Lear.* What, fifty of my followers at a clap?
Within a fortnight?

261 *gall* bitterness 271 *derogate* degraded 272 *teem* increase 273 *spleen*
ill-humor, spitefulness 274 *thwart disnatured* perverse unnatural 276 *cadent* falling *fret* wear 277 *pains and benefits* care and offerings 283 *disposition* mood

Albany.   What's the matter, sir?

Lear. I'll tell thee. *[to Goneril]* Life and death, I am ashamed
That thou hast power to shake my manhood thus!
That these hot tears, which break from me perforce,
Should make thee worth them. Blasts and fogs upon thee! 290
Th' untented woundings of a father's curse
Pierce every sense about thee! Old fond eyes,
Beweep this cause again I'll pluck ye out
And cast you, with the waters that you loose,
To temper clay. [Yea, is it come to this?]   295
Ha! Let it be so. I have another daughter,
Who I am sure is kind and comfortable.
When she shall hear this of thee, with her nails
She'll flay thy wolvish visage. Thou shalt find
That I'll resume the shape which thou dost think   300
I have cast off for ever.

                    Exit [Lear with Kent and Attendants].

Goneril.   Do you mark that?

Albany. I cannot be so partial, Goneril,
To the great love I bear you —

Goneril. Pray you, content. — What, Oswald, ho!
[To Fool] You, sir, more knave than fool, after your
master!   305

Fool. Nuncle Lear, nuncle Lear, tarry. Take the fool with
thee.

            A fox, when one has caught her,
            And such a daughter,
            Should sure to the slaughter,   310

289 *perforce* by force, against my will   291 *untented* untentable, too deep
for treatment by a probe   292 *sense about* faculty possessed by *fond* foolish
293 *Beweep this cause* if you weep over this matter   294 *loose* let loose
295 *temper* soften   297 *comfortable* ready to comfort   300 *shape* i.e. rôle
of authority   302-3 *partial . . . To* made partial . . . by   306 *the fool* i.e.
both your fool and your folly   310 *slaughter* hanging and quartering

                    If my cap would buy a halter.
                    So the fool follows after.   *Exit.*

  Goneril. This man hath had good counsel – a hundred
    knights!
    'Tis politic and safe to let him keep
315 At point a hundred knights – yes, that on every dream,
    Each buzz, each fancy, each complaint, dislike,
    He may enguard his dotage with their pow'rs
    And hold our lives in mercy. – Oswald, I say!
  Albany. Well, you may fear too far.
  Goneril.   Safer than trust too far.
320 Let me still take away the harms I fear,
    Not fear still to be taken. I know his heart.
    What he hath uttered I have writ my sister.
    If she sustain him and his hundred knights,
    When I have showed th' unfitness –

Enter Steward [Oswald].

                       How now, Oswald?
325 What, have you writ that letter to my sister?
  Oswald. Ay, madam.
  Goneril. Take you some company, and away to horse.
    Inform her full of my particular fear,
    And thereto add such reasons of your own
330 As may compact it more. Get you gone,
    And hasten your return. *[Exit Oswald.]* No, no, my lord,
    This milky gentleness and course of yours,
    Though I condemn not, yet under pardon,

311, 312 *halter, after* (pronounced 'hauter,' 'auter') 313 *good counsel* i.e.
from such company (ironic) 314 *politic* prudent 315 *At point* in arms
316 *buzz* murmur 318 *in mercy* at his mercy 320 *still . . . harms* always
eliminate the sources of injury 321 *still . . . taken* always to be overtaken
(by them) 327 *some company* an escort 328 *particular* own 330 *compact
it more* substantiate it further 332 *milky . . . course* mildly gentle way

You are much more ataskéd for want of wisdom
Than praised for harmful mildness.   335
Albany. How far your eyes may pierce I cannot tell;
Striving to better, oft we mar what's well.
Goneril. Nay then —
Albany. Well, well; th' event.   *Exeunt.*

Enter Lear, Kent, and Fool.   I, v

Lear. Go you before to Gloucester with these letters. Acquaint my daughter no further with anything you know than comes from her demand out of the letter. If your diligence be not speedy, I shall be there afore you.

Kent. I will not sleep, my lord, till I have delivered your   5
letter.   *Exit.*

Fool. If a man's brains were in's heels, were't not in danger of kibes?

Lear. Ay, boy.

Fool. Then I prithee be merry. Thy wit shall not go slipshod. 10

Lear. Ha, ha, ha.

Fool. Shalt see thy other daughter will use thee kindly; for though she's as like this as a crab's like an apple, yet I can tell what I can tell.

Lear. What canst tell, boy?   15

Fool. She will taste as like this as a crab does to a crab. Thou canst tell why one's nose stands i' th' middle on's face?

Lear. No.

334 *ataskéd* censured, taken to task   335 *harmful mildness* mildness that proves harmful   339 *th' event* the outcome, i.e. we shall see what happens
I, v, 3 *demand out of* i.e. questioning provoked by reading   8 *kibes* chilblains   10 *wit . . . slipshod* intelligence (brain) shall not go slippered (because of 'kibes')   12 *Shalt* thou shalt   *kindly* after her kind, i.e. in the same way as this daughter   13 *crab* crabapple

Fool. Why, to keep one's eyes of either side 's nose, that
20   what a man cannot smell out he may spy into.

Lear. I did her wrong.

Fool. Canst tell how an oyster makes his shell?

Lear. No.

Fool. Nor I neither; but I can tell why a snail has a house.

25 *Lear.* Why?

Fool. Why, to put 's head in; not to give it away to his
daughters, and leave his horns without a case.

Lear. I will forget my nature. So kind a father! — Be my
horses ready?

30 *Fool.* Thy asses are gone about 'em. The reason why the
seven stars are no moe than seven is a pretty reason.

Lear. Because they are not eight.

Fool. Yes indeed. Thou wouldst make a good fool.

Lear. To take 't again perforce — Monster ingratitude!

35 *Fool.* If thou wert my fool, nuncle, I'ld have thee beaten for
being old before thy time.

Lear. How's that?

Fool. Thou shouldst not have been old till thou hadst been
wise.

40 *Lear.* O, let me not be mad, not mad, sweet heaven!
Keep me in temper; I would not be mad!

[Enter a Gentleman.]

How now, are the horses ready?

Gentleman. Ready, my lord.

Lear. Come, boy.

21 *her* i.e. Cordelia (the first of the remarkable intimations of Lear's
inner thoughts in this scene) 27 *horns* i.e. snail's horns (with pun on
cuckold's horns; the legitimacy of Goneril and Regan being, figuratively,
suspect throughout) *case* covering 28 *nature* i.e. fatherly instincts 31 *moe*
more 34 *perforce* by force 41 *in temper* properly balanced

Fool. She that's a maid now, and laughs at my departure, 45
Shall not be a maid long, unless things be cut shorter.

Exeunt.

Enter Bastard [Edmund] and Curan severally.   II, i

Edmund. Save thee, Curan.

Curan. And you, sir. I have been with your father, and
given him notice that the Duke of Cornwall and Regan
his Duchess will be here with him this night.

Edmund. How comes that?   5

Curan. Nay, I know not. You have heard of the news
abroad — I mean the whispered ones, for they are yet but
ear-kissing arguments?

Edmund. Not I. Pray you, what are they?

Curan. Have you heard of no likely wars toward, 'twixt the 10
Dukes of Cornwall and Albany?

Edmund. Not a word.

Curan. You may do, then, in time. Fare you well, sir. *Exit.*

Edmund. The Duke be here to-night? The better best!
This weaves itself perforce into my business.   15
My father hath set guard to take my brother,
And I have one thing of a queasy question
Which I must act. Briefness and fortune, work!
Brother, a word: descend. Brother, I say!

45-46 *She ... shorter* (an indecent gag addressed to the audience, calculated
to embarrass the maids who joined in the laughter) II, i, 1 *Save* God
save 8 *ear-kissing arguments* whispered topics 10 *likely* probable *toward*
impending 14 *better best* (hyperbole) 15 *perforce* of necessity (?) of its
own accord (?) 17 *of . . . question* delicately balanced as to outcome,
touch-and-go 18 *Briefness and fortune* decisive speed and good luck

Enter Edgar.

20 My father watches. O sir, fly this place.
Intelligence is given where you are hid.
You have now the good advantage of the night.
Have you not spoken 'gainst the Duke of Cornwall?
He's coming hither; now i' th' night, i' th' haste,
25 And Regan with him. Have you nothing said
Upon his party 'gainst the Duke of Albany?
Advise yourself.

Edgar.   I am sure on't, not a word.

Edmund. I hear my father coming. Pardon me:
In cunning I must draw my sword upon you.
30 Draw, seem to defend yourself; now quit you well. —
Yield! Come before my father! Light ho, here! —
Fly, brother. — Torches, torches! — So farewell.

                             Exit Edgar.

Some blood drawn on me would beget opinion
Of my more fierce endeavor. *[Wounds his arm.]* I have
seen drunkards
35 Do more than this in sport. — Father, father!
Stop, stop! No help?

Enter Gloucester, and Servants with torches.

Gloucester. Now, Edmund, where's the villain?

Edmund. Here stood he in the dark, his sharp sword out,
Mumbling of wicked charms, conjuring the moon
To stand auspicious mistress.

40 *Gloucester.*   But where is he?

Edmund. Look, sir, I bleed.

26 *Upon his party 'gainst* i.e. reflecting upon his feud against   27 *Advise
yourself* take thought   *on't* of it   29 *In cunning* i.e. as a ruse   30 *quit you*
acquit yourself

Gloucester.   Where is the villain, Edmund?
Edmund. Fled this way, sir, when by no means he could —
Gloucester. Pursue him, ho! Go after. *[Exeunt some Servants.]*
    By no means what?
Edmund. Persuade me to the murder of your lordship;
    But that I told him the revenging gods   45
    'Gainst parricides did all the thunder bend;
    Spoke with how manifold and strong a bond
    The child was bound to th' father — sir, in fine,
    Seeing how loathly opposite I stood
    To his unnatural purpose, in fell motion   50
    With his preparèd sword he charges home
    My unprovided body, latched mine arm;
    And when he saw my best alarumed spirits
    Bold in the quarrel's right, roused to th' encounter,
    Or whether gasted by the noise I made,   55
    Full suddenly he fled.
Gloucester.   Let him fly far.
    Not in this land shall he remain uncaught;
    And found — dispatch. The noble Duke my master,
    My worthy arch and patron, comes to-night:
    By his authority I will proclaim it   60
    That he which finds him shall deserve our thanks,
    Bringing the murderous coward to the stake;
    He that conceals him, death.
Edmund. When I dissuaded him from his intent
    And found him pight to do it, with curst speech   65
    I threatened to discover him. He replied,

46 *bend* aim   48 *in fine* finally   49 *loathly opposite* in loathing opposition
50 *fell* deadly   52 *unprovided* undefended   *latched* lanced, pierced   53 *best
alarumed* fully aroused   54 *Bold ... right* confident in the justice of the cause
55 *gasted* struck aghast   58 *dispatch* (equivalent to 'death' or 'finis')
59 *arch* superior   65 *pight* determined, set   *curst* angry   66 *discover* expose

'Thou unpossessing bastard; dost thou think,
If I would stand against thee, would the reposal
Of any trust, virtue, or worth in thee
70 Make thy words faithed? No. What I should deny
(As this I would, ay, though thou didst produce
My very character) I'ld turn it all
To thy suggestion, plot, and damnèd practice;
And thou must make a dullard of the world,
75 If they not thought the profits of my death
Were very pregnant and potential spirits
To make thee seek it.'

Gloucester.   O strange and fast'ned villain!
Would he deny his letter, said he? [I never got him.]
             Tucket within.
Hark, the Duke's trumpets. I know not why he comes.
80 All ports I'll bar; the villain shall not 'scape;
The Duke must grant me that. Besides, his picture
I will send far and near, that all the kingdom
May have due note of him; and of my land,
Loyal and natural boy, I'll work the means
85 To make thee capable.

Enter Cornwall, Regan, and Attendants.

Cornwall. How now, my noble friend? Since I came hither
(Which I can call but now) I have heard strange news.

67 *unpossessing* having no claim, landless 68 *reposal* placing 70 *faithed* believed 72 *character* written testimony 73 *suggestion* instigation *practice* devices 74 *make . . . world* i.e. consider everyone stupid 75 *not thought* did not think 76 *pregnant . . . spirits* teeming and powerful spirits, i.e. the devils which 'possess' him 77 *fast'ned* confirmed 78 *got* begot s.D. *Tucket* (personal signature in trumpet notes) 85 *capable* i.e. legitimate, able to inherit 87 *call* i.e. say was

Regan. If it be true, all vengeance comes too short
   Which can pursue th' offender. How dost, my lord?
Gloucester. O madam, my old heart is cracked, it's cracked. 90
Regan. What, did my father's godson seek your life?
   He whom my father named, your Edgar?
Gloucester. O lady, lady, shame would have it hid.
Regan. Was he not companion with the riotous knights
   That tended upon my father?   95
Gloucester. I know not, madam. 'Tis too bad, too bad.
Edmund. Yes, madam, he was of that consort.
Regan. No marvel then though he were ill affected.
   'Tis they have put him on the old man's death,
   To have th' expense and waste of his revenues.   100
   I have this present evening from my sister
   Been well informed of them, and with such cautions
   That, if they come to sojourn at my house,
   I'll not be there.
Cornwall.   Nor I, assure thee, Regan.
   Edmund, I hear that you have shown your father   105
   A childlike office.
Edmund.   It was my duty, sir.
Gloucester. He did bewray his practice, and received
   This hurt you see, striving to apprehend him.
Cornwall. Is he pursued?
Gloucester.   Ay, my good lord.
Cornwall. If he be taken, he shall never more   110
   Be feared of doing harm. Make your own purpose,
   How in my strength you please. For you, Edmund,

---

97 *consort* company, set   98 *affected* disposed   99 *put* set   100 *expense and waste* wasteful expenditure   106 *childlike* filial   107 *bewray his practice* expose his plot   111 *of doing* lest he do   111–12 *Make . . . please* i.e. accomplish your purpose, making free use of my powers

Whose virtue and obedience doth this instant
So much commend itself, you shall be ours.
115 Natures of such deep trust we shall much need;
You we first seize on.
Edmund.   I shall serve you, sir,
Truly, however else.
Gloucester.   For him I thank your Grace.
Cornwall. You know not why we came to visit you?
Regan. Thus out of season, threading dark-eyed night.
120 Occasions, noble Gloucester, of some prize,
Wherein we must have use of your advice.
Our father he hath writ, so hath our sister,
Of differences, which I best thought it fit
To answer from our home. The several messengers
125 From hence attend dispatch. Our good old friend,
Lay comforts to your bosom, and bestow
Your needful counsel to our businesses,
Which craves the instant use.
Gloucester.   I serve you, madam.
Your Graces are right welcome.   *Exeunt. Flourish.*

II, ii   *Enter Kent and Steward [Oswald], severally.*

Oswald. Good dawning to thee, friend. Art of this house?
Kent. Ay.

113 *virtue and obedience* virtuous obedience   120 *prize* price, importance
123 *differences* quarrels   *which* (refers, indefinitely, to the whole situation)
124 *answer . . . home* cope with away from home (where she need not
receive Lear)   125 *attend dispatch* i.e. await settlement of the business
126 *Lay . . . bosom* be consoled (about your own trouble)   127 *needful*
needed   128 *craves . . . use* requires immediate transaction (?) or use of
your counsel (?)   II, ii, 1 *dawning* (perhaps indicating that it is too early for
'good morning')   *Art . . . house* i.e. do you belong to this household

Oswald. Where may we set our horses?

Kent. I' th' mire.

Oswald. Prithee, if thou lov'st me, tell me.   5

Kent. I love thee not.

Oswald. Why then, I care not for thee.

Kent. If I had thee in Lipsbury Pinfold, I would make thee
care for me.

Oswald. Why dost thou use me thus? I know thee not.   10

Kent. Fellow, I know thee.

Oswald. What dost thou know me for?

Kent. A knave, a rascal, an eater of broken meats; a base,
proud, shallow, beggarly, three-suited, hundred-pound,
filthy worsted-stocking knave; a lily-livered, action-tak-   15
ing, whoreson, glass-gazing, superserviceable, finical
rogue; one-trunk-inheriting slave; one that wouldst be a
bawd in way of good service, and art nothing but the
composition of a knave, beggar, coward, pander, and the
son and heir of a mongrel bitch; one whom I will beat   20
into clamorous whining if thou deny'st the least syllable
of thy addition.

Oswald. Why, what a monstrous fellow art thou, thus to
rail on one that is neither known of thee nor knows thee!

Kent. What a brazen-faced varlet art thou to deny thou   25
knowest me! Is it two days ago since I tripped up thy
heels and beat thee before the King? *[Draws his sword.]*
Draw, you rogue, for though it be night, yet the moon

---

8 *Lipsbury Pinfold* i.e. between the teeth (cant term: 'pen in the region of
the lips') 13 *broken meats* scraps 14 *three-suited* with three suits (the
wardrobe allowed serving-men) *hundred-pound* (the minimal estate for
anyone aspiring to gentility) 15 *worsted-stocking* (serving-men's attire)
15–16 *action-taking* i.e. cowardly (resorting to law instead of fighting)
16 *glass-gazing, superserviceable, finical* i.e. conceited, toadying, foppish
17 *inheriting* possessing 17–18 *a bawd . . . service* i.e. a pander, if pleasing
your employer required it 19 *composition* composite 22 *addition* titles

75

shines. I'll make a sop o' th' moonshine of you. You
30   whoreson cullionly barbermonger, draw!
Oswald. Away, I have nothing to do with thee.
Kent. Draw, you rascal. You come with letters against the
      King, and take Vanity the puppet's part against the
      royalty of her father. Draw, you rogue, or I'll so car-
35   bonado your shanks. Draw, you rascal. Come your ways!
Oswald. Help, ho! Murder! Help!
Kent. Strike, you slave! Stand, rogue! Stand, you neat
      slave! Strike!   *[Beats him.]*
Oswald. Help, ho! Murder, murder!

      Enter Bastard [Edmund, with his rapier drawn], Cornwall,
         Regan, Gloucester, Servants.

40 *Edmund.* How now? What's the matter? Part!
Kent. With you, goodman boy, if you please! Come, I'll
      flesh ye; come on, young master.
Gloucester. Weapons? Arms? What's the matter here?
Cornwall. Keep peace, upon your lives.
45   He dies that strikes again. What is the matter?
Regan. The messengers from our sister and the King.
Cornwall. What is your difference? Speak.
Oswald. I am scarce in breath, my lord.
Kent. No marvel, you have so bestirred your valor. You
50   cowardly rascal, nature disclaims in thee. A tailor made
      thee.

---

29 *sop o' th' moonshine* i.e. something that sops up moonshine through its
perforations   30 *cullionly barbermonger* vile fop (i.e. always dealing with
hairdressers)   33 *Vanity the puppet* i.e. Goneril (here equated with a
stock figure in morality plays, now dwindled into puppet shows)   34–35
carbonado dice (like a steak)   35 *your ways* get along   37 *neat* primping
41 *goodman boy* (doubly contemptuous, since peasants were addressed as
'goodmen')   42 *flesh ye* give you your first taste of blood   49 *bestirred*
exercised   50 *disclaims* claims no part

Cornwall. Thou art a strange fellow. A tailor make a man?

Kent. A tailor, sir. A stonecutter or a painter could not have
   made him so ill, though they had been but two years o'
   th' trade.   55

Cornwall. Speak yet, how grew your quarrel?

Oswald. This ancient ruffian, sir, whose life I have spared
   at suit of his gray beard —

Kent. Thou whoreson zed, thou unnecessary letter! My
   lord, if you will give me leave, I will tread this unbolted 60
   villain into mortar and daub the wall of a jakes with him.
   Spare my gray beard? you wagtail.

Cornwall. Peace, sirrah!
   You beastly knave, know you no reverence?

Kent. Yes, sir, but anger hath a privilege.   65

Cornwall. Why art thou angry?

Kent. That such a slave as this should wear a sword,
   Who wears no honesty. Such smiling rogues as these
   Like rats oft bite the holy cords atwain
   Which are too intrinse t' unloose; smooth every
      passion   70
   That in the natures of their lords rebel,
   Being oil to fire, snow to the colder moods;
   Renege, affirm, and turn their halcyon beaks
   With every gale and vary of their masters,
   Knowing naught, like dogs, but following.   75

53 *stonecutter* sculptor 58 *At suit of* on the plea of, moved to mercy by
59 *zed* z (last and least useful of letters) 60 *unbolted* unsifted, crude
61 *jakes* privy 62 *wagtail* (any of several birds whose tail-feathers wag or
bob, suggesting obsequiousness or effeminacy) 64 *beastly* beast-like, ir-
rational 69 *holy cords* sacred bonds (between parents and children, husbands and wives, man and God) 70 *intrinse* intrinsic, inextricable *smooth*
flatter, cater to 71 *rebel* (i.e. against reason and moral restraint) 72 *Being
. . . moods* (i.e. feeders of intemperance) 73 *Renege* deny *halcyon beaks*
kingfisher beaks (supposedly serving as weathervanes when the birds were
hung up by their necks) 74 *gale and vary* varying wind

A plague upon your epileptic visage!
Smile you my speeches, as I were a fool?
Goose, if I had you upon Sarum Plain,
I'ld drive ye cackling home to Camelot.
80 *Cornwall.* What, art thou mad, old fellow?
Gloucester. How fell you out? Say that.
Kent. No contraries hold more antipathy
  Than I and such a knave.
Cornwall. Why dost thou call him knave? What is his fault?
85 *Kent.* His countenance likes me not.
Cornwall. No more perchance does mine, nor his, nor hers.
Kent. Sir, 'tis my occupation to be plain:
  I have seen better faces in my time
  Than stands on any shoulder that I see
  Before me at this instant.
90 *Cornwall.*   This is some fellow
  Who, having been praised for bluntness, doth affect
  A saucy roughness, and constrains the garb
  Quite from his nature. He cannot flatter, he;
  An honest mind and plain – he must speak truth.
95 An they will take it, so; if not, he's plain.
  These kind of knaves I know which in this plainness
  Harbor more craft and more corrupter ends
  Than twenty silly-ducking observants
  That stretch their duties nicely.
100 *Kent.* Sir, in good faith, in sincere verity,

---

76 *epileptic* contorted in a grin (?) 77 *Smile you* smile you at, mock you
78 *Sarum Plain* Salisbury Plain (said to have been associated with geese,
but the allusion remains cryptic) 79 *Camelot* legendary seat of King
Arthur, variously sited at Winchester, near Cadbury, in Wales, etc.
82 *contraries* opposites 92–93 *constrains . . . nature* distorts the plain fashion
from its true nature, caricatures it 98 *silly-ducking observants* ludicrously
bowing form-servers 99 *nicely* fussily

Under th' allowance of your great aspect,
Whose influence, like the wreath of radiant fire
On flick'ring Phoebus' front –
Cornwall.   What mean'st by this?
Kent. To go out of my dialect, which you discommend so
  much. I know, sir, I am no flatterer. He that beguiled you   105
  in a plain accent was a plain knave, which, for my part, I
  will not be, though I should win your displeasure to en-
  treat me to't.
Cornwall. What was th' offense you gave him?
Oswald. I never gave him any.   110
  It pleased the King his master very late
  To strike at me, upon his misconstruction;
  When he, compact, and flattering his displeasure,
  Tripped me behind; being down, insulted, railed,
  And put upon him such a deal of man   115
  That worthied him, got praises of the King
  For him attempting who was self-subdued;
  And, in the fleshment of this dread exploit,
  Drew on me here again.
Kent.   None of these rogues and cowards
  But Ajax is their fool.

---

101 *allowance* approval   *aspect* (1) appearance (2) heavenly position
102 *influence* astrological force   103 *Phoebus' front* sun's forehead (i.e. face)
104 *go . . . dialect* depart from my way of speaking   105 *He* (the type of
plain-speaker Cornwall has condemned)   107–8 *though . . . to't* though I
should persuade your disapproving self to beg me to do so (? with 'displeasure' sarcastically substituted for 'grace')   111 *very late* quite recently
112 *misconstruction* misunderstanding   113 *compact* in league with   115 *And
put . . . man* i.e. affected such excessive manliness   116 *worthied* enhanced
his worth   117 *For him . . . self-subdued* for assailing him (Oswald) who
chose not to resist   118 *fleshment of* bloodthirstiness induced by   119–20
None . . . fool i.e. the Ajax type, stupidly belligerent, is the favorite butt of
cowardly rogues like Oswald

120 *Cornwall.*   Fetch forth the stocks!
You stubborn ancient knave, you reverent braggart,
We'll teach you.
    Kent.   Sir, I am too old to learn.
Call not your stocks for me, I serve the King —
On whose employment I was sent to you;
125 You shall do small respect, show too bold malice
Against the grace and person of my master,
Stocking his messenger.
    Cornwall. Fetch forth the stocks. As I have life and honor,
There shall he sit till noon.
130 *Regan.* Till noon? Till night, my lord, and all night too.
    Kent. Why, madam, if I were your father's dog,
You should not use me so.
    Regan.   Sir, being his knave, I will.
    Cornwall. This is a fellow of the selfsame color
Our sister speaks of. Come, bring away the stocks.
                           Stocks brought out.
135 *Gloucester.* Let me beseech your Grace not to do so.
[His fault is much, and the good King his master
Will check him for't. Your purposed low correction
Is such as basest and contemnèd'st wretches
For pilf'rings and most common trespasses
140 Are punished with.]
The King his master needs must take it ill
That he, so slightly valued in his messenger,
Should have him thus restrained.
    Cornwall.   I'll answer that.
    Regan. My sister may receive it much more worse,

---

121 *Stubborn* rude *reverent* aged 125 *malice* ill will 126 *grace* royal
honor 133 *color* kind 134 *away* along 137 *check* rebuke *purposed*
intended 138 *contemnèd'st* most harshly sentenced 142 *slightly valued in*
i.e. little respected in the person of 143 *answer* answer for

To have her gentleman abused, assaulted,   145
[For following her affairs. Put in his legs.]
                      [Kent is put in the stocks.]

Cornwall. Come, my lord, away!
                Exit [with all but Gloucester and Kent.]

Gloucester. I am sorry for thee, friend. 'Tis the Duke's pleasure,
  Whose disposition all the world well knows
  Will not be rubbed nor stopped. I'll entreat for thee.   150

Kent. Pray do not, sir. I have watched and travelled hard.
  Some time I shall sleep out, the rest I'll whistle.
  A good man's fortune may grow out at heels.
  Give you good morrow.

Gloucester. The Duke's to blame in this. 'Twill be ill taken. 155
                                Exit.

Kent. Good King, that must approve the common saw,
  Thou out of heaven's benediction com'st
  To the warm sun.
  Approach, thou beacon to this under globe,
  That by thy comfortable beams I may   160
  Peruse this letter. Nothing almost sees miracles
  But misery. I know 'tis from Cordelia,
  Who hath most fortunately been informed
  Of my obscurèd course. And shall find time
  From this enormous state, seeking to give   165
  Losses their remedies. – All weary and o'erwatched,

149 *disposition* inclination   150 *rubbed* deflected (bowling term)   151
watched gone sleepless   153 *A good ... heels* i.e. it is no disgrace to decline
in fortune   154 *Give* God give   155 *taken* received   156 *approve* demon-
strate the truth of   *saw* saying, proverb   157–58 *Thou ... sun* (proverb,
meaning from better to worse, i.e. from heavenly shelter to earthly exposure—'the heat of the day')   159 *beacon ... globe* i.e. the sun (here viewed
as benign)   161–62 *Nothing ... misery* i.e. miraculous aid is seldom seen (or
searched for?) except by the miserable   164 *obscurèd* disguised   164–66 *And
... remedies* (incoherent: perhaps corrupt, or perhaps snatches read from
the letter)   165 *enormous state* monstrous situation   166 *Losses* reverses

Take vantage, heavy eyes, not to behold
This shameful lodging. Fortune, good night;
Smile once more, turn thy wheel. *[Sleeps.]*

II, iii *Enter Edgar.*

Edgar. I heard myself proclaimed,
And by the happy hollow of a tree
Escaped the hunt. No port is free, no place
That guard and most unusual vigilance
5 Does not attend my taking. Whiles I may 'scape,
I will preserve myself; and am bethought
To take the basest and most poorest shape
That ever penury, in contempt of man,
Brought near to beast: my face I'll grime with filth,
10 Blanket my loins, elf all my hairs in knots,
And with presented nakedness outface
The winds and persecutions of the sky.
The country gives me proof and precedent
Of Bedlam beggars, who, with roaring voices,
15 Strike in their numbed and mortified bare arms
Pins, wooden pricks, nails, sprigs of rosemary;
And with this horrible object, from low farms,
Poor pelting villages, sheepcotes, and mills,
Sometimes with lunatic bans, sometime with prayers,
20 Enforce their charity. Poor Turlygod, poor Tom,
That's something yet: Edgar I nothing am. *Exit.*

167 *vantage* i.e. advantage of sleep 168 *lodging* (in the stocks) 169 *wheel* (Fortune's wheel was represented as vertical. Kent is at its bottom.) II, iii, 2 *happy hollow* i.e. lucky hiding-place 5 *attend my taking* contemplate my capture 6 *bethought* in mind 10 *elf* tangle (into 'elf-locks') 11 *presented* a show of 13 *proof* example 14 *Bedlam* (see I, ii, 131–32) 15 *Strike* stick *mortified* deadened to pain 16 *pricks* skewers 17 *object* picture 18 *pelting* paltry 19 *bans* curses 20 *Turlygod* (unidentified, but evidently another name for a Tom o' Bedlam) 21 *Edgar* i.e. as Edgar

Enter Lear, Fool, and Gentleman.   II, iv

Lear. 'Tis strange that they should so depart from
      home,
   And not send back my messenger.
Gentleman.   As I learned,
   The night before there was no purpose in them
   Of this remove.
Kent.   Hail to thee, noble master.
Lear. Ha!   5
   Mak'st thou this shame thy pastime?
Kent.   No, my lord.
Fool. Ha, ha, he wears cruel garters. Horses are tied by the
   heads, dogs and bears by th' neck, monkeys by th' loins,
   and men by th' legs. When a man's over-lusty at legs,
   then he wears wooden nether-stocks.   10
Lear. What's he that hath so much thy place mistook
   To set thee here?
Kent.   It is both he and she,
   Your son and daughter.
Lear. No.
Kent. Yes.   15
Lear. No, I say.
Kent. I say yea.
[*Lear.* No, no, they would not.
Kent. Yes, they have.]
Lear. By Jupiter, I swear no!   20
Kent. By Juno, I swear ay!
Lear.   They durst not do't;

II, iv, 3 *purpose* intention   4 *remove* removal   7 *cruel* painful (with pun
on 'crewel,' a yarn used in garters)   9 *over-lusty at legs* i.e. too much on the
go (?) or too much given to kicking (?)   10 *nether-stocks* stockings (as
distinct from 'upper-stocks' or breeches)

They could not, would not do't. 'Tis worse than
   murder
To do upon respect such violent outrage.
Resolve me with all modest haste which way
25   Thou mightst deserve or they impose this usage,
Coming from us.
Kent.   My lord, when at their home
I did commend your Highness' letters to them,
Ere I was risen from the place that showed
My duty kneeling, came there a reeking post,
30   Stewed in his haste, half breathless, panting forth
From Goneril his mistress salutations;
Delivered letters, spite of intermission,
Which presently they read; on whose contents
They summoned up their meiny, straight took horse,
35   Commanded me to follow and attend
The leisure of their answer, gave me cold looks;
And meeting here the other messenger,
Whose welcome I perceived had poisoned mine,
Being the very fellow which of late
40   Displayed so saucily against your Highness,
Having more man than wit about me, drew;
He raised the house with loud and coward cries.
Your son and daughter found this trespass worth
The shame which here it suffers.
45 *Fool.* Winter's not gone yet, if the wild geese fly that way.

23 *To . . . outrage* i.e. to show such outrageous disrespect 24 *Resolve*
enlighten *modest* seemly 27 *commend* entrust 30 *Stewed* steaming
32 *spite of intermission* in disregard of its being an interruption 33 *presently* immediately *on* on the strength of 34 *meiny* attendants 40 *Displayed* showed off 41 *man* manhood *wit* sense 42 *raised* aroused 45
Winter's . . . way i.e. the ill season continues according to these signs (with
Cornwall and Regan equated with 'wild geese,' proverbially evasive)

    Fathers that wear rags
      Do make their children blind,
    But fathers that bear bags
      Shall see their children kind.
    Fortune, that arrant whore,   50
    Ne'er turns the key to th' poor.
But for all this, thou shalt have as many dolors for thy
daughters as thou canst tell in a year.
Lear. O, how this mother swells up toward my heart!
Hysterica passio, down, thou climbing sorrow;   55
Thy element's below. Where is this daughter?
Kent. With the Earl, sir, here within.
Lear.   Follow me not;
   Stay here.   *Exit.*
Gentleman. Made you no more offense but what you speak of?
Kent. None.   60
   How chance the King comes with so small a number?
Fool. An thou hadst been set i' th' stocks for that question,
   thou'dst well deserved it.
Kent. Why, fool?
Fool. We'll set thee to school to an ant, to teach thee there's   65
   no laboring i' th' winter. All that follow their noses are
   led by their eyes but blind men, and there's not a nose
   among twenty but can smell him that's stinking. Let go
   thy hold when a great wheel runs down a hill, lest it break

47 *blind* (to their fathers' needs)   48 *bags* (of gold)   50 *Fortune . . . whore*
(because so fickle and callous)   51 *turns the key* i.e. opens the door   52 *dolors* sorrows (with pun on 'dollars,' continental coins)   53 *tell* count
54, 55 *mother, Hysterica passio* hysteria (the popular and the medical terms)
56 *element* proper place   66 *no laboring . . . winter* (Lear, accompanied by 'so
small a number,' is equated with winter bereft of workers, such as ants.)
66–68 *All . . . stinking* i.e. almost anyone can smell out a person decayed in
fortune

70 thy neck with following. But the great one that goes upward, let him draw thee after. When a wise man gives
thee better counsel, give me mine again. I would have
none but knaves follow it since a fool gives it.
            That sir which serves and seeks for gain,
75   And follows but for form,
            Will pack when it begins to rain
            And leave thee in the storm.
            But I will tarry; the fool will stay,
            And let the wise man fly.
80   The knave turns fool that runs away;
            The fool no knave, perdy.
Kent. Where learned you this, fool?
Fool. Not i' th' stocks, fool.

Enter Lear and Gloucester.

Lear. Deny to speak with me? They are sick, they are
    weary,
85 They have travelled all the night? Mere fetches,
The images of revolt and flying off!
Fetch me a better answer.
Gloucester.   My dear lord,
You know the fiery quality of the Duke,
How unremovable and fixed he is
In his own course.
90 *Lear.*   Vengeance, plague, death, confusion!
Fiery? What quality? Why, Gloucester, Gloucester,
I'ld speak with the Duke of Cornwall and his wife.

73 *none but knaves* (Here and in what follows the Fool repudiates his
advice to abandon Lear.) 75 *form* show 76 *pack* be off 80 *The knave . . .
away* i.e. faithlessness is the true folly 81 *perdy* I swear (from *par dieu*)
83 *fool* (persiflage, but also a term of honor; cf. V, iii, 306) 85 *fetches*
counterfeit reasons, false likenesses of truth 86 *images* true likenesses
flying off revolt 88 *quality* disposition

Gloucester. Well, my good lord, I have informed them so.
Lear. Informed them? Dost thou understand me, man?
Gloucester. Ay, my good lord.   95
Lear. The King would speak with Cornwall. The dear
    father
  Would with his daughter speak, commands – tends –
    service.
  Are they informed of this? My breath and blood!
  Fiery? The fiery Duke, tell the hot Duke that –
  No, but not yet. May be he is not well.   100
  Infirmity doth still neglect all office
  Whereto our health is bound. We are not ourselves
  When nature, being oppressed, commands the mind
  To suffer with the body. I'll forbear;
  And am fallen out with my more headier will   105
  To take the indisposed and sickly fit
  For the sound man. – Death on my state! Wherefore
  Should he sit here? This act persuades me
  That this remotion of the Duke and her
  Is practice only. Give me my servant forth.   110
  Go tell the Duke and's wife I'ld speak with them!
  Now, presently! Bid them come forth and hear me,
  Or at their chamber door I'll beat the drum
  Till it cry sleep to death.
Gloucester. I would have all well betwixt you.   *Exit.*   115
Lear. O me, my heart, my rising heart! But down!
Fool. Cry to it, nuncle, as the cockney did to the eels when
  she put 'em i' th' paste alive. She knapped 'em o' th' cox-

---

97 *tends* attends, awaits (?) or tenders, offers (?)   101 *all office* duties
102 *Whereto . . . bound* to which, in health, we are bound   105 *headier*
headstrong   108 *he* i.e. Kent   109 *remotion* remaining remote, inaccessible   110 *practice* trickery   112 *presently* immediately   114 *cry* pursue
with noise (like a pack or 'cry' of hounds)   117 *cockney* city-dweller
118 *paste* pastry pie   *knapped* rapped

combs with a stick and cried, 'Down, wantons, down!'
120 'Twas her brother that, in pure kindness to his horse,
buttered his hay.

Enter Cornwall, Regan, Gloucester, Servants.

Lear. Good morrow to you both.
Cornwall.   Hail to your Grace.
                                         Kent here set at liberty.
Regan. I am glad to see your Highness.
Lear. Regan, I think you are. I know what reason
125 I have to think so. If thou shouldst not be glad,
I would divorce me from thy mother's tomb,
Sepulchring an adultress. *[to Kent]* O, are you free?
Some other time for that. — Beloved Regan,
Thy sister 's naught. O Regan, she hath tied
130 Sharp-toothed unkindness, like a vulture, here.
I can scarce speak to thee. Thou'lt not believe
With how depraved a quality — O Regan!
Regan. I pray you, sir, take patience. I have hope
You less know how to value her desert
Than she to scant her duty.
135 *Lear.*   Say? how is that?
Regan. I cannot think my sister in the least
Would fail her obligation. If, sir, perchance
She have restrained the riots of your followers,
'Tis on such ground, and to such wholesome end,
140 As clears her from all blame.
Lear. My curses on her!

119 *wantons* i.e. frisky things   121 *buttered his hay* (another example of
rustic humor at the expense of cockney inexperience)   126–27 *divorce . . .
adultress* i.e. refuse to be buried with your mother since such a child as you
must have been conceived in adultery   132 *how . . . quality* i.e. what innate
depravity   133 *have hope* i.e. suspect   135 *scant* (in effect, a double nega-
tive; 'do' would be more logical though less emphatic)

Regan.   O, sir, you are old;
  Nature in you stands on the very verge
  Of his confine. You should be ruled, and led
  By some discretion that discerns your state
  Better than you yourself. Therefore I pray you   145
  That to our sister you do make return;
  Say you have wronged her.
Lear.   Ask her forgiveness?
  Do you but mark how this becomes the house:
  'Dear daughter, I confess that I am old.   *[Kneels.]*
  Age is unnecessary. On my knees I beg   150
  That you'll vouchsafe me raiment, bed, and food.'
Regan. Good sir, no more. These are unsightly tricks.
  Return you to my sister.
Lear.   *[rises]* Never, Regan.
  She hath abated me of half my train,
  Looked black upon me, struck me with her tongue   155
  Most serpent-like upon the very heart.
  All the stored vengeances of heaven fall
  On her ingrateful top! Strike her young bones,
  You taking airs, with lameness.
Cornwall.   Fie, sir, fie!
Lear. You nimble lightnings, dart your blinding flames   160
  Into her scornful eyes! Infect her beauty,
  You fen-sucked fogs drawn by the pow'rful sun
  To fall and blister.
Regan.   O the blest gods!
  So will you wish on me when the rash mood is on.

142–43 *Nature . . . confine* i.e. your life nears the limit of its tenure 144
some discretion . . . state someone discerning enough to recognize your condition 148 *the house* household or family decorum 154 *abated* curtailed
158 *ingrateful top* ungrateful head 159 *taking* infectious 162 *fen-sucked*
drawn up from swamps 163 *fall and blister* strike and raise blisters (such
as those of smallpox)

165 *Lear.* No, Regan, thou shalt never have my curse.
        Thy tender-hefted nature shall not give
        Thee o'er to harshness. Her eyes are fierce, but thine
        Do comfort, and not burn. 'Tis not in thee
        To grudge my pleasures, to cut off my train,
170   To bandy hasty words, to scant my sizes,
        And, in conclusion, to oppose the bolt
        Against my coming in. Thou better know'st
        The offices of nature, bond of childhood,
        Effects of courtesy, dues of gratitude.
175   Thy half o' th' kingdom hast thou not forgot,
        Wherein I thee endowed.
Regan.   Good sir, to th' purpose.
                                        Tucket within.

Lear. Who put my man i' th' stocks?
Cornwall.   What trumpet's that?
Regan. I know't — my sister's. This approves her letter,
        That she would soon be here.

                Enter Steward [Oswald].

                                Is your lady come?
180 *Lear.* This is a slave, whose easy-borrowèd pride
        Dwells in the fickle grace of her he follows.
        Out, varlet, from my sight.
Cornwall.   What means your Grace?
Lear. Who stocked my servant? Regan, I have good
        hope
        Thou didst not know on't.

166 *tender-hefted* swayed by tenderness, gently disposed   170 *bandy* volley
sizes allowances   171 *oppose the bolt* i.e. bar the door   173 *offices of nature*
natural duties   174 *Effects* actions   176 *purpose* point   178 *approves* con-
firms   180 *easy-borrowèd* acquired on small security   181 *grace* favor
182 *varlet* low fellow

Enter Goneril.

                              Who comes here? O heavens!
If you do love old men, if your sweet sway   185
Allow obedience, if you yourselves are old,
Make it your cause. Send down, and take my part.
[To Goneril] Art not ashamed to look upon this beard?
O Regan, will you take her by the hand?
Goneril. Why not by th' hand, sir? How have I offended? 190
All's not offense that indiscretion finds
And dotage terms so.
Lear.   O sides, you are too tough!
Will you yet hold? How came my man i' th' stocks?
Cornwall. I set him there, sir; but his own disorders
Deserved much less advancement.
Lear.   You? Did you?   195
Regan. I pray you, father, being weak, seem so.
If till the expiration of your month
You will return and sojourn with my sister,
Dismissing half your train, come then to me.
I am now from home, and out of that provision   200
Which shall be needful for your entertainment.
Lear. Return to her, and fifty men dismissed?
No, rather I abjure all roofs, and choose
To wage against the enmity o' th' air,
To be a comrade with the wolf and owl,   205
Necessity's sharp pinch. Return with her?
Why, the hot-blooded France, that dowerless took

186 *Allow* approve 187 *Make ... cause* i.e. make my cause yours 191 *indiscretion finds* ill judgment detects as such 192 *sides* breast (which should burst with grief) 195 *less advancement* i.e. more abasement 196 *seem so* i.e. act the part 201 *entertainment* lodging 204 *wage* fight 206 *Necessity's sharp pinch* (a summing up of the hardships previously listed) 207 *hot-blooded* choleric (cf. I, ii, 23)

Our youngest born, I could as well be brought
To knee his throne, and, squire-like, pension beg
210 To keep base life afoot. Return with her?
Persuade me rather to be slave and sumpter
To this detested groom.
Goneril.   At your choice, sir.
Lear. I prithee, daughter, do not make me mad.
I will not trouble thee, my child; farewell.
215 We'll no more meet, no more see one another.
But yet thou art my flesh, my blood, my daughter;
Or rather a disease that's in my flesh,
Which I must needs call mine. Thou art a boil,
A plague-sore, or embossèd carbuncle
220 In my corrupted blood. But I'll not chide thee.
Let shame come when it will, I do not call it.
I do not bid the thunder-bearer shoot,
Nor tell tales of thee to high-judging Jove.
Mend when thou canst, be better at thy leisure;
225 I can be patient, I can stay with Regan,
I and my hundred knights.
Regan.   Not altogether so.
I looked not for you yet, nor am provided
For your fit welcome. Give ear, sir, to my sister;
For those that mingle reason with your passion
230 Must be content to think you old, and so —
But she knows what she does.
Lear.   Is this well spoken?
Regan. I dare avouch it, sir. What, fifty followers?
Is it not well? What should you need of more?

209 *knee* kneel at   *squire-like* like an attendant   211 *sumpter* packhorse
212 *groom* i.e. Oswald   219 *embossèd* risen to a head   222 *thunder-bearer*
i.e. Jupiter   223 *high-judging* judging from on high   229 *mingle ... passion*
interpret your passion in the light of reason   232 *avouch* swear by

Yea, or so many, sith that both charge and danger
Speak 'gainst so great a number? How in one house   235
Should many people, under two commands,
Hold amity? 'Tis hard, almost impossible.
Goneril. Why might not you, my lord, receive attendance
From those that she calls servants, or from mine?
Regan. Why not, my lord? If then they chanced to slack ye,   240
We could control them. If you will come to me
(For now I spy a danger), I entreat you
To bring but five-and-twenty. To no more
Will I give place or notice.
Lear. I gave you all.
Regan.   And in good time you gave it.   245
Lear. Made you my guardians, my depositaries,
But kept a reservation to be followèd
With such a number. What, must I come to you
With five-and-twenty? Regan, said you so?
Regan. And speak't again, my lord. No more with me.   250
Lear. Those wicked creatures yet do look well-favored
When others are more wicked; not being the worst
Stands in some rank of praise. *[to Goneril]* I'll go with
    thee.
Thy fifty yet doth double five-and-twenty,
And thou art twice her love.
Goneril.   Hear me, my lord.   255
What need you five-and-twenty? ten? or five?
To follow in a house where twice so many
Have a command to tend you?
Regan.   What need one?

---

234 *sith that* since *charge* expense 240 *slack* neglect 244 *notice* recognition 246 *depositaries* trustees 247 *kept . . . to be* stipulated that I be
251 *well-favored* comely 253 *Stands . . . praise* i.e. is at least relatively
praiseworthy 255 *her love* i.e. as loving as she

Lear. O reason not the need! Our basest beggars
260   Are in the poorest thing superfluous.
Allow not nature more than nature needs,
Man's life is cheap as beast's. Thou art a lady:
If only to go warm were gorgeous,
Why, nature needs not what thou gorgeous wear'st,
265   Which scarcely keeps thee warm. But, for true need —
You heavens, give me that patience, patience I need.
You see me here, you gods, a poor old man,
As full of grief as age, wretched in both.
If it be you that stirs these daughters' hearts
270   Against their father, fool me not so much
To bear it tamely; touch me with noble anger,
And let not women's weapons, water drops,
Stain my man's cheeks. No, you unnatural hags!
I will have such revenges on you both
275   That all the world shall — I will do such things —
What they are, yet I know not; but they shall be
The terrors of the earth. You think I'll weep.
No, I'll not weep.   *Storm and tempest.*
I have full cause of weeping, but this heart
280   Shall break into a hundred thousand flaws
Or ere I'll weep. O fool, I shall go mad!
          Exeunt [Lear, Fool, Kent, and Gloucester].
Cornwall. Let us withdraw; 'twill be a storm.
Regan. This house is little; the old man and 's people
Cannot be well bestowed.

259 *reason* analyze 260 *Are . . . superfluous* i.e. have some poor possession not utterly indispensable 261 *than nature needs* i.e. than life needs for mere survival 263-65 *If . . . warm* i.e. if to be dressed warmly (i.e. for need) were considered sufficiently gorgeous, you would not need your present attire, which is gorgeous rather than warm 270 *fool* play with, humiliate 280 *flaws* fragments 281 *Or ere* before

Goneril. 'Tis his own blame; hath put himself from rest   285
 And must needs taste his folly.
Regan. For his particular, I'll receive him gladly,
 But not one follower.
Goneril.   So am I purposed.
 Where is my Lord of Gloucester?
Cornwall. Followèd the old man forth.

Enter Gloucester.

                              He is returned.   290

Gloucester. The King is in high rage.
Cornwall.   Whither is he going?
Gloucester. He calls to horse, but will I know not whither.
Cornwall. 'Tis best to give him way; he leads himself.
Goneril. My lord, entreat him by no means to stay.
Gloucester. Alack, the night comes on, and the high winds 295
 Do sorely ruffle. For many miles about
 There's scarce a bush.
Regan.   O, sir, to willful men
 The injuries that they themselves procure
 Must be their schoolmasters. Shut up your doors.
 He is attended with a desperate train,   300
 And what they may incense him to, being apt
 To have his ear abused, wisdom bids fear.
Cornwall. Shut up your doors, my lord; 'tis a wild night.
 My Regan counsels well. Come out o' th' storm. *Exeunt.*

285 *hath . . . rest* i.e. he himself is responsible for leaving his resting place
with her (?) or, he is self-afflicted (?) 287 *particular* own person 288 *purposed* determined 296 *ruffle* rage 301-2 *apt . . . abused* i.e. predisposed
to listen to ill counsel

III, i   *Storm still. Enter Kent and a Gentleman severally.*

Kent. Who's there besides foul weather?
Gentleman. One minded like the weather, most unquietly.
Kent. I know you. Where's the King?
Gentleman. Contending with the fretful elements;
5   Bids the wind blow the earth into the sea,
       Or swell the curlèd waters 'bove the main,
       That things might change or cease; [tears his white hair,
       Which the impetuous blasts, with eyeless rage,
       Catch in their fury and make nothing of;
10   Strives in his little world of man to outscorn
       The to-and-fro-conflicting wind and rain.
       This night, wherein the cub-drawn bear would couch,
       The lion and the belly-pinchèd wolf
       Keep their fur dry, unbonneted he runs,
       And bids what will take all.]
15 *Kent.*   But who is with him?
Gentleman. None but the fool, who labors to outjest
       His heart-struck injuries.
Kent.   Sir, I do know you,
       And dare upon the warrant of my note
       Commend a dear thing to you. There is division,
20   Although as yet the face of it is covered
       With mutual cunning, 'twixt Albany and Cornwall;
       Who have — as who have not, that their great stars

III, i, 2 *minded . . . unquietly* i.e. in disturbed mood   4 *Contending* quarrelling   6 *main* mainland   7 *change* revert to chaos (?) or, improve (?)   8 *eyeless* (1) blind (2) invisible   10 *little world* (the 'microcosm,' which is disturbed like the great world or 'macrocosm')   12 *cub-drawn* cubsucked (and hence ravenous)   13 *belly-pinchèd* famished   15 *take all* (the cry of the desperate gambler in staking his last)   18 *warrant . . . note* assurance of my knowledge   19 *Commend . . . thing* entrust a precious matter   22 *that* whom   *stars* destinies

Throned and set high? — servants, who seem no less,
Which are to France the spies and speculations
Intelligent of our state. What hath been seen,   25
Either in snuffs and packings of the Dukes,
Or the hard rein which both of them have borne
Against the old kind King, or something deeper,
Whereof, perchance, these are but furnishings —
[But, true it is, from France there comes a power   30
Into this scatterèd kingdom, who already,
Wise in our negligence, have secret feet
In some of our best ports and are at point
To show their open banner. Now to you:
If on my credit you dare build so far   35
To make your speed to Dover, you shall find
Some that will thank you, making just report
Of how unnatural and bemadding sorrow
The King hath cause to plain.
I am a gentleman of blood and breeding,   40
And from some knowledge and assurance offer
This office to you.]
Gentleman. I will talk further with you.
Kent.   No, do not.
For confirmation that I am much more
Than my out-wall, open this purse and take   45
What it contains. If you shall see Cordelia,
As fear not but you shall, show her this ring,
And she will tell you who that fellow is

23 *Throned* have throned *no less* i.e. truly so 24 *speculations* spies 25 *Intelligent* supplying intelligence 26 *snuffs* quarrels *packings* intrigues 27 *hard rein . . . borne* i.e. harsh curbs . . . exercised 29 *furnishings* pretexts 30 *power* army 31 *scatterèd* divided 35 *my credit* trust in me *build* take constructive action 38 *bemadding sorrow* maddening grievances 39 *plain* lament 42 *office* service 45 *out-wall* surface appearance

That yet you do not know. Fie on this storm!
50 I will go seek the King.
   Gentleman. Give me your hand. Have you no more to say?
   Kent. Few words, but, to effect, more than all yet:
     That when we have found the King – in which your pain
     That way, I'll this – he that first lights on him
55   Holla the other.   *Exeunt [severally].*

III, ii   *Storm still. Enter Lear and Fool.*

   Lear. Blow, winds, and crack your cheeks. Rage, blow.
     You cataracts and hurricanoes, spout
     Till you have drenched our steeples, drowned the cocks.
     You sulph'rous and thought-executing fires,
5   Vaunt-couriers to oak-cleaving thunderbolts,
     Singe my white head. And thou, all-shaking thunder,
     Strike flat the thick rotundity o' th' world,
     Crack Nature's moulds, all germains spill at once,
     That makes ingrateful man.
10 *Fool.* O nuncle, court holy-water in a dry house is better
     than this rain water out o' door. Good nuncle, in; ask thy
     daughters blessing. Here's a night pities neither wise men
     nor fools.
   Lear. Rumble thy bellyful. Spit, fire. Spout, rain.
15 Nor rain, wind, thunder, fire are my daughters.
     I tax not you, you elements, with unkindness.
     I never gave you kingdom, called you children;

52 *to effect* in their import   53 *pain* pains, care   III, ii, 2 *hurricanoes* water-
spouts   3 *cocks* weathercocks   4 *thought-executing fires* i.e. flashes of lightning swift as thought (?) or, dazing, benumbing the mind (?)   5 *Vaunt-*
couriers heralds   8 *moulds* (in which Nature's creations are formed)   *ger-*
mains seeds   10 *court holy-water* flattery (slang)   16 *tax* charge

You owe me no subscription. Then let fall
Your horrible pleasure. Here I stand your slave,
A poor, infirm, weak, and despised old man.   20
But yet I call you servile ministers,
That will with two pernicious daughters join
Your high-engendered battles 'gainst a head
So old and white as this. O, ho! 'tis foul.

Fool. He that has a house to put 's head in has a good head- 25
piece.

> The codpiece that will house
> Before the head has any,
> The head and he shall louse:
> So beggars marry many.   30
> The man that makes his toe
> What he his heart should make
> Shall of a corn cry woe,
> And turn his sleep to wake.

For there was never yet fair woman but she made mouths 35
in a glass.

Enter Kent.

Lear. No, I will be the pattern of all patience;
I will say nothing.
Kent. Who's there?

18 *subscription* deference   19 *pleasure* will   21 *ministers* agents   23 *high-engendered battles* heavenly battalions   27–30 *The codpiece . . . many* (The moral of the rime is that improvident cohabitation spells penury.)   27 *cod-piece* padded gusset at the crotch of the trunks (slang for 'phallus')   29 *he* it   30 *many* (head-lice and body-lice, accompanying poverty)   31–34 *The man . . . wake* (a parallel instance of misery deriving from reckless impulse: to transpose the tender and precious heart and the tough and base toe is to invite injury; with 'heart' also suggesting Cordelia)   35–36 *made . . . glass* i.e. posed before a mirror (irrelevant, except as vanity is a form of folly, the Fool's general theme)

40 *Fool.* Marry, here's grace and a codpiece; that's a wise man
   and a fool.
   Kent. Alas, sir, are you here? Things that love night
   Love not such nights as these. The wrathful skies
   Gallow the very wanderers of the dark
45 And make them keep their caves. Since I was man,
   Such sheets of fire, such bursts of horrid thunder,
   Such groans of roaring wind and rain, I never
   Remember to have heard. Man's nature cannot carry
   Th' affliction nor the fear.
   Lear.   Let the great gods
50 That keep this dreadful pudder o'er our heads
   Find out their enemies now. Tremble, thou wretch,
   That hast within thee undivulgèd crimes
   Unwhipped of justice. Hide thee, thou bloody hand,
   Thou perjured, and thou simular of virtue
55 That art incestuous. Caitiff, to pieces shake,
   That under covert and convenient seeming
   Has practiced on man's life. Close pent-up guilts,
   Rive your concealing continents and cry
   These dreadful summoners grace. I am a man
   More sinned against than sinning.
60 *Kent.*   Alack, bareheaded?
   Gracious my lord, hard by here is a hovel;
   Some friendship will it lend you 'gainst the tempest.
   Repose you there, while I to this hard house
   (More harder than the stones whereof 'tis raised,

---

44 *Gallow* frighten 45 *keep their caves* i.e. keep under cover 46 *horrid*
horrible 48 *carry* bear 50 *pudder* turmoil 51 *Find . . . enemies* i.e. discover sinners (by their show of fear) 54 *simular* counterfeit 56 *seeming*
hypocrisy 57 *practiced on* plotted against *Close* secret 58 *Rive* split,
break through *continents* containers, covers 59 *summoners* arresting officers of ecclesiastical courts *grace* mercy 61 *Gracious my lord* my gracious
lord 63 *house* household (both building and occupants)

Which even but now, demanding after you,   65
Denied me to come in) return, and force
Their scanted courtesy.
Lear.   My wits begin to turn.
Come on, my boy. How dost, my boy? Art cold?
I am cold myself. Where is this straw, my fellow?
The art of our necessities is strange,   70
And can make vile things precious. Come, your hovel.
Poor fool and knave, I have one part in my heart
That's sorry yet for thee.
Fool. [*sings*]
      He that has and a little tiny wit,
         With, heigh-ho, the wind and the rain,   75
      Must make content with his fortunes fit
         Though the rain it raineth every day.
Lear. True, boy. Come, bring us to this hovel.
                         Exit [*with Kent*].
Fool. This is a brave night to cool a courtesan. I'll speak a
   prophecy ere I go: 80
      When priests are more in word than matter;
      When brewers mar their malt with water;
      When nobles are their tailors' tutors,
      No heretics burned, but wenches' suitors;
      When every case in law is right,   85
      No squire in debt nor no poor knight;
      When slanders do not live in tongues,

---

65 *demanding after* inquiring for   67 *scanted* stinted   70 *art* magic skill
(as in alchemy)   76 *make . . . fit* i.e. reconcile himself to his fortunes
79 *brave* fine   81 *are . . . matter* i.e. can outshine the gospel message (At
present their ability to speak is quite unworthy of their theme.)   82 *mar* i.e.
dilute (At present they dilute water with malt, producing very small beer.)
83 *are . . . tutors* i.e. are no longer subservient to fashion (Each subsequent
line also reverses the present state of affairs.)   84 *burned* (pun on contract-
ing venereal disease)   *wenches' suitors* i.e. libertines

Nor cutpurses come not to throngs;
When usurers tell their gold i' th' field,
90 And bawds and whores do churches build —
Then shall the realm of Albion
Come to great confusion.
Then comes the time, who lives to see't,
That going shall be used with feet.
95 ` This prophecy Merlin shall make, for I live before his
time.   *Exit.*

III, iii   *Enter Gloucester and Edmund.*

Gloucester. Alack, alack, Edmund, I like not this unnatural
dealing. When I desired their leave that I might pity him,
they took from me the use of mine own house, charged
me on pain of perpetual displeasure neither to speak of
5 him, entreat for him, or any way sustain him.
Edmund. Most savage and unnatural.
Gloucester. Go to; say you nothing. There is division between the Dukes, and a worse matter than that. I have
received a letter this night — 'tis dangerous to be spoken —
10 I have locked the letter in my closet. These injuries the
King now bears will be revenged home; there is part of a
power already footed; we must incline to the King. I will
look him and privily relieve him. Go you and maintain

89 *tell* count *i' th' field* (instead of in secret places) 91 *Albion* England
92 *confusion* ruin (ironic: an edifice of abuses is 'ruined' by reform)
94 *going . . . feet* walking will be done with feet (the humor of anticlimax,
but suggesting a return to normality) 95 *Merlin* (a legendary magician
associated with King Arthur, who reigned later than King Lear) III, iii, 2
pity have mercy upon 5 *entreat* plead 7 *division* contention 8 *worse* more
serious 10 *closet* chamber 11 *home* thoroughly 12 *power* army *footed*
landed *incline to* side with 13 *look* search for *privily* secretly

talk with the Duke, that my charity be not of him perceived. If he ask for me, I am ill and gone to bed. If I die 15
for it, as no less is threatened me, the King my old master
must be relieved. There is strange things toward, Edmund; pray you be careful.   *Exit.*

Edmund. This courtesy forbid thee shall the Duke
Instantly know, and of that letter too.   20
This seems a fair deserving, and must draw me
That which my father loses — no less than all.
The younger rises when the old doth fall.   *Exit.*

Enter Lear, Kent, and Fool.   III, iv

Kent. Here is the place, my lord. Good my lord, enter.
The tyranny of the open night's too rough
For nature to endure.   *Storm still.*
Lear.   Let me alone.
Kent. Good my lord, enter here.
Lear.   Wilt break my heart?
Kent. I had rather break mine own. Good my lord, enter. 5
Lear. Thou think'st 'tis much that this contentious storm
Invades us to the skin. So 'tis to thee,
But where the greater malady is fixed
The lesser is scarce felt. Thou'dst shun a bear;
But if thy flight lay toward the roaring sea,   10
Thou'dst meet the bear i' th' mouth. When the mind's
free,

---

17 *toward* imminent **19** *courtesy* kind attention (to Lear) **21** *fair deserving*
i.e. action that should win favor III, iv, **1** *Good my lord* my good lord
4 *break my heart* i.e. by removing the distraction of mere physical distress
8 *fixed* lodged **11** *i' th' mouth* i.e. in the teeth *free* free of care

The body's delicate. The tempest in my mind
Doth from my senses take all feeling else
Save what beats there. Filial ingratitude,
15   Is it not as this mouth should tear this hand
For lifting food to't? But I will punish home.
No, I will weep no more. In such a night
To shut me out! Pour on; I will endure.
In such a night as this! O Regan, Goneril,
20   Your old kind father, whose frank heart gave all —
O, that way madness lies; let me shun that.
No more of that.
Kent.   Good my lord, enter here
Lear. Prithee go in thyself; seek thine own ease.
This tempest will not give me leave to ponder
25   On things would hurt me more, but I'll go in.
[To the Fool] In, boy; go first. You houseless poverty —
Nay, get thee in. I'll pray, and then I'll sleep.   Exit [Fool].
Poor naked wretches, wheresoe'er you are,
That bide the pelting of this pitiless storm,
30   How shall your houseless heads and unfed sides,
Your looped and windowed raggedness, defend you
From seasons such as these? O, I have ta'en
Too little care of this! Take physic, pomp;
Expose thyself to feel what wretches feel,
35   That thou mayst shake the superflux to them
And show the heavens more just.
Edgar. [within] Fathom and half, fathom and half! Poor
Tom!

16 *home* i.e. to the hilt   20 *frank* liberal   26 *houseless* unsheltered   31
looped loopholed   33 *Take physic, pomp* i.e. cure yourself, you vainglori-
ous ones   35 *superflux* superfluities   37 *Fathom and half* (nautical cry in
taking soundings, perhaps suggested by the deluge)

Enter Fool.

Fool. Come not in here, nuncle; here's a spirit. Help me,
  help me!   40
Kent. Give me thy hand. Who's there?
Fool. A spirit, a spirit. He says his name's poor Tom.
Kent. What art thou that dost grumble there i' th' straw?
  Come forth.

Enter Edgar [as Tom o' Bedlam].

Edgar. Away! the foul fiend follows me. Through the 45
  sharp hawthorn blow the winds. Humh! go to thy bed,
  and warm thee.
Lear. Didst thou give all to thy daughters? And art thou
  come to this?
Edgar. Who gives anything to poor Tom? whom the foul 50
  fiend hath led through fire and through flame, through
  ford and whirlpool, o'er bog and quagmire; that hath
  laid knives under his pillow and halters in his pew, set
  ratsbane by his porridge, made him proud of heart, to
  ride on a bay trotting horse over four-inched bridges, to 55
  course his own shadow for a traitor. Bless thy five wits,
  Tom's acold. O, do, de, do, de, do, de. Bless thee from
  whirlwinds, star-blasting, and taking. Do poor Tom
  some charity, whom the foul fiend vexes. There could I
  have him now – and there – and there again – and there – 60
                                           Storm still.

45–46 *Through . . . winds* (cf. ll. 93–94; a line from a ballad) 46–47 *go . . .
thee* (evidently a popular retort; cf. *Taming of the Shrew*, Induction, I, 10)
53–54 *knives, halters, ratsbane* (temptations to suicide) 53 *pew* a gallery
or balcony 55 *ride . . . bridges* i.e. take mad risks 56 *course . . . traitor*
chase his own shadow as an enemy 58 *star-blasting* i.e. becoming the
victim of malignant stars *taking* pestilence

Lear. Has his daughters brought him to this pass?
   Couldst thou save nothing? Wouldst thou give 'em
   all?
Fool. Nay, he reserved a blanket, else we had been all
   shamed.
65 *Lear.* Now all the plagues that in the pendulous air
   Hang fated o'er men's faults light on thy daughters!
Kent. He hath no daughters, sir.
Lear. Death, traitor; nothing could have subdued nature
   To such a lowness but his unkind daughters.
70 Is it the fashion that discarded fathers
   Should have thus little mercy on their flesh?
   Judicious punishment — 'twas this flesh begot
   Those pelican daughters.
Edgar. Pillicock sat on Pillicock Hill. Alow, alow, loo, loo!
75 *Fool.* This cold night will turn us all to fools and madmen.
Edgar. Take heed o' th' foul fiend; obey thy parents; keep
   thy words' justice; swear not; commit not with man's
   sworn spouse; set not thy sweet heart on proud array.
   Tom's acold.
80 *Lear.* What hast thou been?
Edgar. A servingman, proud in heart and mind; that curled
   my hair, wore gloves in my cap; served the lust of my
   mistress' heart, and did the act of darkness with her; swore
   as many oaths as I spake words, and broke them in the

---

61 *pass* evil condition   63 *blanket* (to cover his nakedness)   65 *pendulous*
ominously suspended   66 *Hang . . . faults* i.e. destined to chastise sins
71 *have . . . flesh* i.e. torture themselves   73 *pelican* i.e. feeding upon the
parent's blood (a supposed habit of this species of bird)   74 *Pillicock . . .
Hill* (probably from a nursery rime; 'Pillicock' is a pet-name for a child)
Alow . . . loo (hunting cry ?)   77 *justice* i.e. dependability   *commit not* (i.e.
adultery)   82 *gloves . . . cap* (a fashion with Elizabethan gallants)

sweet face of heaven. One that slept in the contriving of 85
lust, and waked to do it. Wine loved I deeply, dice dearly;
and in woman out-paramoured the Turk. False of heart,
light of ear, bloody of hand; hog in sloth, fox in stealth,
wolf in greediness, dog in madness, lion in prey. Let not
the creaking of shoes nor the rustling of silks betray thy 90
poor heart to woman. Keep thy foot out of brothels, thy
hand out of plackets, thy pen from lenders' books, and
defy the foul fiend. Still through the hawthorn blows the
cold wind; says suum, mun, nonny. Dolphin my boy,
boy, sessa! let him trot by.   *Storm still.* 95

Lear. Thou wert better in a grave than to answer with thy
uncovered body this extremity of the skies. Is man no
more than this? Consider him well. Thou ow'st the
worm no silk, the beast no hide, the sheep no wool, the
cat no perfume. Ha! here's three on's are sophisticated. 100
Thou art the thing itself; unaccommodated man is no
more but such a poor, bare, forked animal as thou art.
Off, off, you lendings! Come, unbutton here.

                              [Begins to disrobe.]

Fool. Prithee, nuncle, be contented; 'tis a naughty night to
swim in. Now a little fire in a wild field were like an old 105
lecher's heart — a small spark, all the rest on's body cold.
Look, here comes a walking fire.

---

87 *out-paramoured the Turk* outdid the Sultan in mistress-keeping 88 *light
of ear* i.e. attentive to flattery and slander 90 *creaking, rustling* (both considered seductively fashionable sounds) 92 *plackets* slits in skirts *pen . . .
books* (in signing for loans) 94 *suum . . . nonny* (the refrain of the wind ?)
94-95 *Dolphin . . . trot by* (variously explained as cant phrases or ballad
refrain, equivalent to 'Let it go') 96 *answer* bear the brunt of 98 *ow'st*
have borrowed from 100 *cat* civet cat *sophisticated* altered by artifice
101 *unaccommodated* unpampered 102 *forked* two-legged 103 *lendings*
borrowed coverings 104 *naughty* evil 105 *wild* barren

Enter Gloucester with a torch.

Edgar. This is the foul Flibbertigibbet. He begins at curfew, and walks till the first cock. He gives the web and the pin,
110 squints the eye, and makes the harelip; mildews the white wheat, and hurts the poor creature of earth.

Swithold footed thrice the 'old;

He met the nightmare, and her nine fold;

Bid her alight

115 And her troth plight,

And aroint thee, witch, aroint thee!

Kent. How fares your Grace?

Lear. What's he?

Kent. Who's there? What is't you seek?

120 *Gloucester.* What are you there? Your names?

Edgar. Poor Tom, that eats the swimming frog, the toad, the todpole, the wall-newt and the water; that in the fury of his heart, when the foul fiend rages, eats cow-dung for sallets, swallows the old rat and the ditch-dog, drinks the
125 green mantle of the standing pool; who is whipped from tithing to tithing, and stock-punished and imprisoned; who hath had three suits to his back, six shirts to his body,

Horse to ride, and weapon to wear,

---

108 *Flibbertigibbet* (a dancing devil) *curfew* (9 p.m.) 109 *first cock* (midnight) *web . . . pin* cataract of the eye 110 *squints* crosses *white* ripening 112 *Swithold* St. Withold (Anglo-Saxon exorcist) *footed* walked over *'old* wold, uplands 113 *nightmare* incubus, demon *fold* offspring 114 *alight* i.e. from the horse she was afflicting 115 *her troth plight* plight her troth, pledge her good intentions 116 *aroint thee* be gone (a direct command, concluding the charm) 122 *todpole* tadpole *water* water-newt 124 *sallets* salads *ditch-dog* (carcass) 125 *mantle* scum *standing* stagnant 126 *tithing* a ten-family district within a parish *stock-punished* placed in the stocks

108

But mice and rats, and such small deer,   130
  Have been Tom's food for seven long year.
Beware my follower! Peace, Smulkin, peace, thou fiend!
Gloucester. What, hath your Grace no better company?
Edgar. The prince of darkness is a gentleman.
  Modo he's called, and Mahu.   135
Gloucester. Our flesh and blood, my lord, is grown so vile
  That it doth hate what gets it.
Edgar. Poor Tom's acold.
Gloucester. Go in with me. My duty cannot suffer
  T' obey in all your daughters' hard commands.   140
  Though their injunction be to bar my doors
  And let this tyrannous night take hold upon you,
  Yet have I ventured to come seek you out
  And bring you where both fire and food is ready.
Lear. First let me talk with this philosopher.   145
  What is the cause of thunder?
Kent. Good my lord, take his offer; go into th' house.
Lear. I'll talk a word with this same learnèd Theban.
  What is your study?
Edgar. How to prevent the fiend, and to kill vermin.   150
Lear. Let me ask you one word in private.
Kent. Importune him once more to go, my lord.
  His wits begin t' unsettle.
Gloucester.   Canst thou blame him?
                                    Storm still.
His daughters seek his death. Ah, that good Kent,

---

130 *deer* game (adapted from lines in the romance *Bevis of Hampton*)
132, 135 *Smulkin, Modo, Mahu* (devils described in Harsnett's *Declaration,*
1603) 137 *gets* begets (a reference to Edgar, Goneril, and Regan) 139 *suffer* permit 148 *Theban* (an unexplained association of Thebes with phi-
losophy, i.e. science) 149 *study* i.e. scientific specialty 150 *prevent* thwart

155 He said it would be thus, poor banished man!
Thou say'st the King grows mad — I'll tell thee, friend,
I am almost mad myself. I had a son,
Now outlawed from my blood; he sought my life
But lately, very late. I loved him, friend,
160 No father his son dearer. True to tell thee,
The grief hath crazed my wits. What a night 's this!
I do beseech your Grace —

Lear.   O, cry you mercy, sir.
Noble philosopher, your company.

Edgar. Tom's acold.

165 *Gloucester.* In, fellow, there, into th' hovel; keep thee warm.

Lear. Come, let's in all.

Kent.   This way, my lord.

Lear.   With him!
I will keep still with my philosopher.

Kent. Good my lord, soothe him; let him take the fellow.

Gloucester. Take him you on.

170 *Kent.* Sirrah, come on; go along with us.

Lear. Come, good Athenian.

Gloucester. No words, no words! Hush.

Edgar.   Child Rowland to the dark tower came;
His word was still, 'Fie, foh, and fum,
175   I smell the blood of a British man.'   *Exeunt.*

158 *outlawed . . . blood* proscribed as no child of mine   162 *cry you mercy*
I beg your pardon   168 *soothe* humor   169 *you on* along with you
171 *Athenian* i.e. philosopher   173 *Child* (i.e. a candidate for knighthood)
Rowland Roland of the Charlemagne legends (the line perhaps from a
lost ballad)   174 *His word was still* i.e. his repeated word, his motto, was
always   174-75 *Fie . . . man* (absurdly heroic)

Enter Cornwall and Edmund.   III, v

Cornwall. I will have my revenge ere I depart his house.

Edmund. How, my lord, I may be censured, that nature thus
  gives way to loyalty, something fears me to think of.

Cornwall. I now perceive it was not altogether your brother's evil disposition made him seek his death; but a pro-   5
  voking merit, set awork by a reproveable badness in
  himself.

Edmund. How malicious is my fortune that I must repent to
  be just! This is the letter which he spoke of, which approves him an intelligent party to the advantages of   10
  France. O heavens, that this treason were not! or not I the
  detector!

Cornwall. Go with me to the Duchess.

Edmund. If the matter of this paper be certain, you have
  mighty business in hand.   15

Cornwall. True or false, it hath made thee Earl of Gloucester. Seek out where thy father is, that he may be ready
  for our apprehension.

Edmund. [aside] If I find him comforting the King, it will
  stuff his suspicion more fully. — I will persever in my   20
  course of loyalty, though the conflict be sore between
  that and my blood.

Cornwall. I will lay trust upon thee, and thou shalt find a
  dearer father in my love.   *Exeunt.*

III, v, 2 *censured* judged   3 *something fears me* frightens me somewhat
5–7 *a provoking . . . himself* i.e. evil justice incited by evil (a case of poison
driving out poison)   9–10 *approves* proves   10 *intelligent . . . advantages*
spying partisan on behalf of   19 *comforting* aiding   20 *persever* persevere
22 *blood* natural feelings   23 *lay . . . thee* trust you(?) reward you with a
place of trust(?)

Enter Kent and Gloucester.

Gloucester. Here is better than the open air; take it thank-
   fully. I will piece out the comfort with what addition I
   can. I will not be long from you.
Kent. All the power of his wits have given way to his im-
5 patience. The gods reward your kindness.

                                          Exit [Gloucester].

                Enter Lear, Edgar, and Fool.

Edgar. Frateretto calls me, and tells me Nero is an angler in
   the lake of darkness. Pray, innocent, and beware the foul
   fiend.
Fool. Prithee, nuncle, tell me whether a madman be a
10 gentleman or a yeoman.
Lear. A king, a king.
Fool. No, he's a yeoman that has a gentleman to his son; for
   he's a mad yeoman that sees his son a gentleman before
   him.
15 *Lear.* To have a thousand with red burning spits
      Come hizzing in upon 'em —
   [*Edgar.* The foul fiend bites my back.
Fool. He's mad that trusts in the tameness of a wolf, a
   horse's health, a boy's love, or a whore's oath.
20 *Lear.* It shall be done; I will arraign them straight.
      [*To Edgar*] Come, sit thou here, most learned justice.
      [*To the Fool*] Thou, sapient sir, sit here. Now, you she-
      foxes —

III, vi, 4–5 *impatience* rage   6 *Frateretto* (a devil mentioned in Harsnett's
Declaration) *Nero* (In Rabelais, Trajan was the angler, Nero a fiddler, in
Hades.)   7 *innocent* hapless victim, plaything   10 *yeoman* a property owner,
next in rank to a gentleman (The allusion is to self-penalizing indulgence
of one's children.)   13 *sees* i.e. sees to it   16 *hizzing* hissing (Lear is musing
on vicious military retaliation.)   20 *arraign* bring to trial

Edgar. Look, where he stands and glares. Want'st thou eyes
  at trial, madam?
         Come o'er the bourn, Bessy, to me.   25
Fool.   Her boat hath a leak,
        And she must not speak
      Why she dares not come over to thee.
Edgar. The foul fiend haunts poor Tom in the voice of a
  nightingale. Hoppedance cries in Tom's belly for two 30
  white herring. Croak not, black angel; I have no food for
  thee.
Kent. How do you, sir? Stand you not so amazed.
  Will you lie down and rest upon the cushions?
Lear. I'll see their trial first. Bring in their evidence. 35
  [To Edgar] Thou, robèd man of justice, take thy place.
  [To the Fool] And thou, his yokefellow of equity,
  Bench by his side. *[to Kent]* You are o' th' commission;
  Sit you too.
Edgar. Let us deal justly.   40
      Sleepest or wakest thou, jolly shepherd?
        Thy sheep be in the corn;
      And for one blast of thy minikin mouth
        Thy sheep shall take no harm.
  Purr, the cat is gray.   45
Lear. Arraign her first. 'Tis Goneril, I here take my oath be-
  fore this honorable assembly, kicked the poor King her
  father.

---

23 *he* Lear (?) or one of Edgar's 'devils' (?)   *eyes* such eyes (?) or spec-
tators (?)   25 *bourn* brook (Edgar's line is from a popular song; the Fool's
are a ribald improvisation.)   30 *nightingale* i.e. the fool *Hoppedance* (a
devil mentioned in Harsnett's *Declaration* as 'Hobberdidance')   31 *white*
unsmoked (in contrast with 'black angel,' i.e. smoked devil)   33 *amazed*
bewildered   38 *commission* those commissioned as King's justices   42 *corn*
wheatfield   43 *one . . . mouth* one strain on your delicate shepherd's pipe (?)
45 *gray* (Gray cats were among the forms supposedly assumed by devils.)

Fool. Come hither, mistress. Is your name Goneril?
50 *Lear.* She cannot deny it.
Fool. Cry you mercy, I took you for a joint-stool.
Lear. And here's another, whose warped looks proclaim
    What store her heart is made on. Stop her there!
    Arms, arms, sword, fire! Corruption in the place!
55   False justicer, why hast thou let her 'scape?]
Edgar. Bless thy five wits!
Kent. O pity! Sir, where is the patience now
    That you so oft have boasted to retain?
Edgar. *[aside]* My tears begin to take his part so much
60   They mar my counterfeiting.
Lear. The little dogs and all,
    Tray, Blanch, and Sweetheart — see, they bark at me.
Edgar. Tom will throw his head at them. Avaunt, you curs.
        Be thy mouth or black or white,
65   Tooth that poisons if it bite;
        Mastiff, greyhound, mongrel grim,
        Hound or spaniel, brach or lym,
        Or bobtail tike, or trundle-tail —
        Tom will make him weep and wail;
70   For, with throwing thus my head,
        Dogs leaped the hatch, and all are fled.
    Do, de, de, de. Sessa! Come, march to wakes and fairs
    and market towns. Poor Tom, thy horn is dry.

51 *Cry . . . joint-stool* (a cant expression for 'Pardon me for failing to notice you,' but two joint-stools—cf. 'warped,' l. 52—were probably the actual stage objects arraigned as Goneril and Regan) 54 *Corruption . . . place* i.e. bribery in the court 59 *take his part* i.e. fall on his behalf 60 *counterfeiting* i.e. simulating madness 67 *brach* hound bitch *lym* bloodhound 68 *Bobtail . . . trundle-tail* short-tailed cur or long-tailed 71 *hatch* lower half of a 'Dutch door' 72 *Sessa* (interjection, equivalent to 'Away!') *wakes* parish feasts 73 *Poor . . . dry* (Edgar expresses his exhaustion in his rôle, by an allusion to the horns proffered by Tom o' Bedlams in begging drink.)

Lear. Then let them anatomize Regan. See what breeds
about her heart. Is there any cause in nature that makes 75
these hard hearts? *[to Edgar]* You, sir, I entertain for one
of my hundred; only I do not like the fashion of your
garments. You will say they are Persian; but let them be
changed.

Kent. Now, good my lord, lie here and rest awhile.   80

Lear. Make no noise, make no noise; draw the curtains.
So, so. We'll go to supper i' th' morning.

Fool. And I'll go to bed at noon.

Enter Gloucester.

Gloucester. Come hither, friend. Where is the King my
    master?

Kent. Here, sir, but trouble him not; his wits are gone. 85

Gloucester. Good friend, I prithee take him in thy arms.
    I have o'erheard a plot of death upon him.
    There is a litter ready; lay him in't
    And drive toward Dover, friend, where thou shalt meet
    Both welcome and protection. Take up thy master.   90
    If thou shouldst dally half an hour, his life,
    With thine and all that offer to defend him,
    Stand in assurèd loss. Take up, take up,
    And follow me, that will to some provision
    Give thee quick conduct.

[*Kent.*   Oppressèd nature sleeps.   95
    This rest might yet have balmed thy broken sinews,
    Which, if convenience will not allow,

78 *Persian* (Persian costume was reputedly gorgeous. Ironically, or in
actual delusion, Lear refers thus to Edgar's rags, as he refers to bed curtains
in l. 81.) 94 *provision* supplies 95 *conduct* guidance 96 *balmed* healed
sinews nerves 97 *convenience* propitious circumstances

Stand in hard cure. *[to the Fool]* Come, help to bear thy
    master.
Thou must not stay behind.]
Gloucester.   Come, come, away!
                                    Exeunt [all but Edgar].

100 [*Edgar.* When we our betters see bearing our woes,
      We scarcely think our miseries our foes.
      Who alone suffers suffers most i' th' mind,
      Leaving free things and happy shows behind;
      But then the mind much sufferance doth o'erskip
105   When grief hath mates, and bearing fellowship.
      How light and portable my pain seems now,
      When that which makes me bend makes the King bow.
      He childed as I fatherèd. Tom, away.
      Mark the high noises, and thyself bewray
110   When false opinion, whose wrong thoughts defile thee,
      In thy just proof repeals and reconciles thee.
      What will hap more to-night, safe 'scape the King!
      Lurk, lurk.]   *[Exit.]*

98 *Stand . . . cure* will be hard to cure 100 *our woes* woes like ours 101 *our foes* i.e. our peculiar foes (They seem rather a part of universal misery.) 103 *free* carefree *shows* scenes 104 *sufferance* suffering 105 *bearing fellowship* enduring has company 106 *portable* bearable 109 *Mark . . . noises* i.e. heed the rumors concerning those in power (?) *bewray* reveal 110 *wrong thoughts* misconceptions 111 *In . . . reconciles thee* i.e. upon your vindication recalls you and makes peace with you 112 *What . . . more* whatever more happens 113 *Lurk* i.e. keep covered

Enter Cornwall, Regan, Goneril, Bastard [Edmund], and   III, vii
  Servants.

Cornwall. *[to Goneril]* Post speedily to my lord your husband; show him this letter. The army of France is landed.
  [to Servants] Seek out the traitor Gloucester.
                              [Exeunt some Servants.]
Regan. Hang him instantly.
Goneril. Pluck out his eyes.   5
Cornwall. Leave him to my displeasure. Edmund, keep you
  our sister company. The revenges we are bound to take
  upon your traitorous father are not fit for your beholding.
  Advise the Duke where you are going, to a most festinate
  preparation. We are bound to the like. Our posts shall be 10
  swift and intelligent betwixt us. Farewell, dear sister;
  farewell, my Lord of Gloucester.

                 Enter Steward [Oswald].

How now? Where's the King?
Oswald. My Lord of Gloucester hath conveyed him hence.
  Some five or six and thirty of his knights,   15
  Hot questrists after him, met him at gate;
  Who, with some other of the lord's dependants,
  Are gone with him toward Dover, where they boast
  To have well-armèd friends.
Cornwall.   Get horses for your mistress.
                              Exit [Oswald].
Goneril. Farewell, sweet lord, and sister.   20

III, vii, 7 *bound* required 9 *festinate* speedy 11 *intelligent* informative
12 *Lord of Gloucester* (as now endowed with his father's title and estates)
16 *questrists* seekers

Cornwall. Edmund, farewell.

                   [Exeunt Goneril and Edmund.]
                   Go seek the traitor Gloucester,
Pinion him like a thief, bring him before us.

                   [Exeunt other Servants.]
Though well we may not pass upon his life
Without the form of justice, yet our power
25   Shall do a court'sy to our wrath, which men
May blame, but not control.

           Enter Gloucester and Servants.

                   Who's there, the traitor?
Regan. Ingrateful fox, 'tis he.
Cornwall. Bind fast his corky arms.
Gloucester. What means your Graces? Good my friends, consider
30   You are my guests. Do me no foul play, friends.
Cornwall. Bind him, I say.   *[Servants bind him.]*
Regan.   Hard, hard! O filthy traitor.
Gloucester. Unmerciful lady as you are, I'm none.
Cornwall. To this chair bind him. Villain, thou shalt find —
                 [Regan plucks his beard.]
Gloucester. By the kind gods, 'tis most ignobly done
35   To pluck me by the beard.
Regan. So white, and such a traitor?
Gloucester.   Naughty lady,
These hairs which thou dost ravish from my chin
Will quicken and accuse thee. I am your host.
With robber's hands my hospitable favors
40   You should not ruffle thus. What will you do?

23 *pass upon* issue a sentence against   25 *do a court'sy to* i.e. defer to, act in
conformity with   28 *corky* (because aged)   36 *Naughty* evil   38 *quicken*
come to life   39 *favors* features   40 *ruffle* tear at

Cornwall. Come, sir, what letters had you late from France?

Regan. Be simple-answered, for we know the truth.

Cornwall. And what confederacy have you with the traitors
    Late footed in the kingdom?

Regan. To whose hands you have sent the lunatic King.   45
    Speak.

Gloucester. I have a letter guessingly set down,
    Which came from one that's of a neutral heart,
    And not from one opposed.

Cornwall.   Cunning.

Regan.   And false.

Cornwall. Where hast thou sent the king?   50

Gloucester. To Dover.

Regan. Wherefore to Dover? Wast thou not charged at
    peril —

Cornwall. Wherefore to Dover? Let him answer that.

Gloucester. I am tied to th' stake, and I must stand the
    course.

Regan. Wherefore to Dover?   55

Gloucester. Because I would not see thy cruel nails
    Pluck out his poor old eyes; nor thy fierce sister
    In his anointed flesh stick boarish fangs.
    The sea, with such a storm as his bare head
    In hell-black night endured, would have buoyed up   60
    And quenched the stellèd fires.
    Yet, poor old heart, he holp the heavens to rain.
    If wolves had at thy gate howled that stern time,
    Thou shouldst have said, 'Good porter, turn the key.'

---

41 *late* of late   42 *Be simple-answered* i.e. give plain answers   44 *footed*
landed   47 *guessingly* i.e. tentatively, not stated as an assured fact   52
charged at peril ordered on peril of your life   54 *course* coursing (as by a
string of dogs baiting a bear or bull tied in the pit)   58 *anointed* (as king)
60 *buoyed* surged   61 *stellèd* starry   62 *holp* helped   64 *turn the key* i.e.
let them come in to shelter

65 All cruels else subscribe. But I shall see
    The wingèd vengeance overtake such children.
Cornwall. See't shalt thou never. Fellows, hold the chair.
    Upon these eyes of thine I'll set my foot.
Gloucester. He that will think to live till he be old,
70 Give me some help. — O cruel! O ye gods!
Regan. One side will mock another. Th' other too.
Cornwall. If you see vengeance —
    1. Servant.   Hold your hand, my lord!
    I have served you ever since I was a child;
    But better service have I never done you
    Than now to bid you hold.
75 *Regan.*   How now, you dog?
    1. Servant. If you did wear a beard upon your chin,
    I'ld shake it on this quarrel. What do you mean!
Cornwall. My villain!   *[Draw and fight.]*
    1. Servant. Nay, then, come on, and take the chance of
       anger.
80 *Regan.* Give me thy sword. A peasant stand up thus?
                [She takes a sword and runs at him behind,] kills him.
    1. Servant. O, I am slain! My lord, you have one eye left
    To see some mischief on him. O!
Cornwall. Lest it see more, prevent it. Out, vile jelly.
    Where is thy lustre now?
Gloucester. All dark and comfortless. Where's my son Ed-
85   mund?

65 *All . . . subscribe* i.e. at such times all other cruel creatures give way,
agree to renounce their cruelty (?) 66 *wingèd* heavenly (?) or swift (?)
69 *will think* hopes, expects 71 *mock* i.e. subject to ridicule (because
of the contrast) 77 *shake it* (as Regan has done with Gloucester's—an
act of extreme defiance) *on this quarrel* in this cause *What . . . mean* i.e.
how dare you (The words are given to Regan by most editors, but they
are no more 'un-servantlike' than those that precede them.) 78 *My villain*
i.e. my serf (with play on its more modern meaning) 82 *mischief* injury

Edmund, enkindle all the sparks of nature
To quit this horrid act.
Regan.   Out, treacherous villain;
Thou call'st on him that hates thee. It was he
That made the overture of thy treasons to us;
Who is too good to pity thee.   90
Gloucester. O my follies! Then Edgar was abused.
Kind gods, forgive me that, and prosper him.
Regan. Go thrust him out at gates, and let him smell
His way to Dover.   *Exit [one] with Gloucester.*
                  How is't, my lord? How look you?
Cornwall. I have received a hurt. Follow me, lady.   95
Turn out that eyeless villain. Throw this slave
Upon the dunghill. Regan, I bleed apace.
Untimely comes this hurt. Give me your arm.   *Exeunt.*
[2. *Servant.* I'll never care what wickedness I do,
If this man come to good.
3. *Servant.*   If she live long,   100
And in the end meet the old course of death,
Women will all turn monsters.
2. *Servant.* Let's follow the old Earl, and get the bedlam
To lead him where he would. His roguish madness
Allows itself to anything.   [*Exit.*] 105
3. *Servant.* Go thou. I'll fetch some flax and whites of eggs
To apply to his bleeding face. Now heaven help him.
                                        Exit.]

86 *nature* natural feeling 87 *quit* requite, avenge *horrid* horrible 89 *over-*
ture disclosure 91 *abused* wronged 94 *How look you* i.e. how looks it with
you, what is your condition 101 *meet . . . death* i.e. die a natural death
104–5 *his roguish . . . anything* i.e. his being an irresponsible wanderer
allows him to do anything

IV, i   *Enter Edgar.*

Edgar. Yet better thus, and known to be contemned,
    Than still contemned and flattered. To be worst,
    The lowest and most dejected thing of fortune,
    Stands still in esperance, lives not in fear.
5   The lamentable change is from the best;
    The worst returns to laughter. Welcome then,
    Thou unsubstantial air that I embrace:
    The wretch that thou hast blown unto the worst
    Owes nothing to thy blasts.

                    Enter Gloucester and an Old Man.

                                          But who comes here?
10 My father, poorly led? World, world, O world!
    But that thy strange mutations make us hate thee,
    Life would not yield to age.
Old Man.   O my good lord,
    I have been your tenant, and your father's tenant,
    These fourscore years.
15 *Gloucester.* Away, get thee away. Good friend, be gone.
    Thy comforts can do me no good at all;
    Thee they may hurt.
Old Man.   You cannot see your way.
Gloucester. I have no way, and therefore want no eyes;
    I stumbled when I saw. Full oft 'tis seen

IV, i, 1 *contemned* despised 3 *dejected* cast down, abased 4 *esperance* hope
6 *The worst . . . laughter* i.e. the worst extreme is the point of return to
happiness 9 *nothing* i.e. nothing good (and hence he is free of debt)
10 *poorly* poor-like, i.e. like a blind beggar (?) 11–12 *But . . . age* i.e.
were it not for your hateful mutability, we would never be reconciled to
old age and death 16 *comforts* ministrations 17 *hurt* do injury (since they
are forbidden) 18 *want* need

Our means secure us, and our mere defects   20
Prove our commodities. O dear son Edgar,
The food of thy abusèd father's wrath,
Might I but live to see thee in my touch
I'ld say I had eyes again!
Old Man.   How now? Who's there?
Edgar. [aside] O gods! Who is't can say 'I am at the worst'? 25
I am worse than e'er I was.
Old Man.   'Tis poor mad Tom.
Edgar. [aside] And worse I may be yet. The worst is not
So long as we can say 'This is the worst.'
Old Man. Fellow, where goest?
Gloucester.   Is it a beggarman?
Old Man. Madman and beggar too.   30
Gloucester. He has some reason, else he could not beg.
I' th' last night's storm I such a fellow saw,
Which made me think a man a worm. My son
Came then into my mind, and yet my mind
Was then scarce friends with him. I have heard more
    since.   35
As flies to wanton boys are we to th' gods;
They kill us for their sport.
Edgar.   *[aside]* How should this be?
Bad is the trade that must play fool to sorrow,
Ang'ring itself and others. — Bless thee, master.
Gloucester. Is that the naked fellow?
Old Man.   Ay, my lord.   40
Gloucester. Get thee away. If for my sake

20-21 *Our means . . . commodities* i.e. prosperity makes us rash, and sheer
affliction proves a boon 22 *food* i.e. the object fed upon *abusèd* deceived
23 *in* i.e. by means of 27-28 *The worst . . . worst* (because at the very
worst there will be no such comforting thought) 31 *reason* powers of
reason 33-34 *My son . . . mind* (because it was actually he—a natural
touch) 36 *wanton* irresponsibly playful 39 *Ang'ring* offending

Thou wilt o'ertake us hence a mile or twain
I' th' way toward Dover, do it for ancient love;
And bring some covering for this naked soul,
Which I'll entreat to lead me.
45 *Old Man.*   Alack, sir, he is mad.
Gloucester. 'Tis the time's plague when madmen lead the
  blind.
Do as I bid thee, or rather do thy pleasure.
Above the rest, be gone.
Old Man. I'll bring him the best 'parel that I have,
50 Come on't what will.   *Exit.*
Gloucester. Sirrah naked fellow —
Edgar. Poor Tom's acold. *[aside]* I cannot daub it further.
Gloucester. Come hither, fellow.
Edgar. *[aside]* And yet I must. — Bless thy sweet eyes, they
  bleed.
55 *Gloucester.* Know'st thou the way to Dover?
Edgar. Both stile and gate, horseway and footpath. Poor
  Tom hath been scared out of his good wits. Bless thee,
  good man's son, from the foul fiend. [Five fiends have
  been in poor Tom at once: of lust, as Obidicut; Hobbidi-
60 dence, prince of dumbness; Mahu, of stealing; Modo,
  of murder; Flibbertigibbet, of mopping and mowing,
  who since possesses chambermaids and waiting women.
  So, bless thee, master.]
Gloucester. Here, take this purse, thou whom the heavens'
  plagues

43 *ancient love* i.e. such love as formerly bound master and man (nostalgic)
46 *time's plague* i.e. malady characteristic of these times   47 *thy pleasure*
as you please   49 *'parel* apparel   52 *daub it* lay it on, act the part   59 *Obidicut* Hoberdicut (a devil mentioned in Harsnett's *Declaration,* as are the
four following)   60 *dumbness* muteness (Shakespeare identifies each devil
with some form of possession.)   61 *mopping and mowing* grimaces, affected
facial expressions

Have humbled to all strokes. That I am wretched   65
Makes thee the happier. Heavens, deal so still!
Let the superfluous and lust-dieted man,
That slaves your ordinance, that will not see
Because he does not feel, feel your pow'r quickly;
So distribution should undo excess,   70
And each man have enough. Dost thou know Dover?
Edgar. Ay, master.
Gloucester. There is a cliff, whose high and bending head
  Looks fearfully in the confinèd deep.
  Bring me but to the very brim of it,   75
  And I'll repair the misery thou dost bear
  With something rich about me. From that place
  I shall no leading need.
Edgar.   Give me thy arm.
  Poor Tom shall lead thee.   *Exeunt.*

Enter Goneril, Bastard [Edmund], and Steward [Oswald].   IV, ii

Goneril. Welcome, my lord. I marvel our mild husband
  Not met us on the way. *[to Oswald]* Now, where's your
    master?
Oswald. Madam, within, but never man so changed.
  I told him of the army that was landed:
  He smiled at it. I told him you were coming: 5
  His answer was, 'The worse.' Of Gloucester's treachery

65 *humbled to* reduced to bearing humbly 66 *happier* i.e. less wretched
67 *superfluous* possessed of superfluities *lust-dieted* i.e. whose desires are
feasted 68 *slaves your ordinance* subordinates your injunction (to share)
73 *bending* overhanging 74 *in . . . deep* i.e. to the sea hemmed in below
IV, ii, 2 *Not met* has not met

And of the loyal service of his son
When I informed him, then he called me sot
And told me I had turned the wrong side out.
10 What most he should dislike seems pleasant to him;
What like, offensive.

Goneril.   [*to Edmund*] Then shall you go no further.
It is the cowish terror of his spirit,
That dares not undertake. He'll not feel wrongs
Which tie him to an answer. Our wishes on the way
15 May prove effects. Back, Edmund, to my brother.
Hasten his musters and conduct his pow'rs.
I must change names at home, and give the distaff
Into my husband's hands. This trusty servant
Shall pass between us. Ere long you are like to hear
20 (If you dare venture in your own behalf)
A mistress's command. Wear this. Spare speech.
                                                  [*Gives a favor.*]
Decline your head. This kiss, if it durst speak,
Would stretch thy spirits up into the air.
Conceive, and fare thee well.

Edmund. Yours in the ranks of death.   *Exit.*
25 *Goneril.*   My most dear Gloucester.
O, the difference of man and man:
To thee a woman's services are due;
My fool usurps my body.

Oswald.   Madam, here comes my lord.   [*Exit.*]

8 *sot* fool 11 *What like* what he should like 12 *cowish* cowardly 13 *undertake* engage 14 *an answer* retaliation 14–15 *Our wishes . . . effects* i.e.
our wishes, that you might supplant Albany, may materialize 16 *musters*
enlistments *conduct his pow'rs* lead his army 17 *change names* i.e. exchange
the name of 'mistress' for 'master' *distaff* spinning-staff (symbol of the
housewife) 21 *mistress's* (At present she plays the rôle of master, but,
mated with Edmund, she would again 'change names.') 24 *Conceive* (1)
understand (2) quicken (with the seed I have planted in you) 28 *usurps*
wrongfully occupies

Enter Albany.

Goneril. I have been worth the whistle.
Albany.   O Goneril,
  You are not worth the dust which the rude wind   30
  Blows in your face. [I fear your disposition:
  That nature which contemns its origin
  Cannot be bordered certain in itself.
  She that herself will sliver and disbranch
  From her material sap, perforce must wither   35
  And come to deadly use.
Goneril. No more; the text is foolish.
Albany. Wisdom and goodness to the vile seem vile;
  Filths savor but themselves. What have you done?
  Tigers not daughters, what have you performed?   40
  A father, and a gracious agèd man,
  Whose reverence even the head-lugged bear would lick,
  Most barbarous, most degenerate, have you madded.
  Could my good brother suffer you to do it?
  A man, a prince, by him so benefited!   45
  If that the heavens do not their visible spirits
  Send quickly down to tame these vile offenses,
  It will come,
  Humanity must perforce prey on itself,
  Like monsters of the deep.]
Goneril.   Milk-livered man,   50

---

29 *worth the whistle* i.e. valued enough to be welcomed home ('not worth
the whistle' applying proverbially to a 'poor dog')   31 *fear your disposition*
distrust your nature   33 *bordered certain* safely contained (It will be unpre-
dictably licentious.)   34 *sliver, disbranch* cut off   35 *material sap* sustaining
stock, nourishing trunk   39 *savor* relish   42 *head-lugged* dragged with a
head-chain (hence, surly)   *lick* i.e. treat with affection   43 *degenerate* unnatural   *madded* maddened   46 *visible* made visible, material   48 *It* i.e.
chaos   50 *Milk-livered* i.e. spiritless

That bear'st a cheek for blows, a head for wrongs;
Who hast not in thy brows an eye discerning
Thine honor from thy suffering; [that not know'st
Fools do those villains pity who are punished
55 Ere they have done their mischief. Where's thy drum?
France spreads his banners in our noiseless land,
With plumèd helm thy state begins to threat,
Whilst thou, a moral fool, sits still and cries
'Alack, why does he so?']
Albany.   See thyself, devil:
60 Proper deformity seems not in the fiend
So horrid as in woman.
Goneril.   O vain fool!
[*Albany.* Thou changèd and self-covered thing, for shame
Bemonster not thy feature. Were't my fitness
To let these hands obey my blood,
65 They are apt enough to dislocate and tear
Thy flesh and bones. Howe'er thou art a fiend,
A woman's shape doth shield thee.
Goneril. Marry, your manhood – mew!]

Enter a Messenger.

[*Albany.* What news?]
70 *Messenger.* O, my good lord, the Duke of Cornwall's dead,

52–53 *discerning . . . suffering* distinguishing between dishonor and tolerance
54 *Fools* i.e. only fools. 55 *drum* i.e. military preparation 56 *noiseless*
i.e. unaroused 57 *helm* war-helmet 58 *moral* moralizing 60 *Proper* i.e.
fair-surfaced 62 *changèd* transformed (diabolically, as in witchcraft)
self-covered i.e. your natural self overwhelmed by evil (?) or devil disguised
as woman (?) 63 *Bemonster . . . feature* i.e. do not exchange your human
features for a monster's *my fitness* fit for me 64 *blood* passion 68 *Marry*
(oath, derived from 'By Mary') *your manhood—mew* i.e. 'What a man!'
followed by a contemptuous interjection (?) or mew up (contain) this
display of manliness

Slain by his servant, going to put out
The other eye of Gloucester.
Albany.   Gloucester's eyes?
Messenger. A servant that he bred, thrilled with remorse,
  Opposed against the act, bending his sword
  To his great master; who, thereat enraged,   75
  Flew on him, and amongst them felled him dead;
  But not without that harmful stroke which since
  Hath plucked him after.
Albany.   This shows you are above,
  You justicers, that these our nether crimes
  So speedily can venge. But, O poor Gloucester,   80
  Lost he his other eye?
Messenger.   Both, both, my lord.
  This letter, madam, craves a speedy answer.
  'Tis from your sister.
Goneril.   [*aside*] One way I like this well;
  But being widow, and my Gloucester with her,
  May all the building in my fancy pluck   85
  Upon my hateful life. Another way
  The news is not so tart. — I'll read, and answer.   [*Exit.*]
Albany. Where was his son when they did take his eyes?
Messenger. Come with my lady hither.
Albany.   He is not here.
Messenger. No, my good lord; I met him back again.   90
Albany. Knows he the wickedness?

---

71 *going to* about to   73 *bred* reared   *thrilled with remorse* in the throes
of pity   76 *amongst them* i.e. aided by the others   78 *plucked him after*
drawn him along (to death)   79 *justicers* dispensers of justice   *nether crimes*
sins committed here below   80 *venge* avenge   82 *craves* requires   85–86
May . . . life i.e. may make my life hateful by destroying my dream-castles
86 *Another way* the other way (alluded to in l. 83, probably the removal
of Cornwall as an obstacle to sole reign with Edmund)   87 *tart* distasteful
90 *back* going back

Messenger. Ay, my good lord. 'Twas he informed against
    him,
    And quit the house on purpose, that their punishment
    Might have the freer course.
Albany.   Gloucester, I live
95   To thank thee for the love thou showed'st the King,
    And to revenge thine eyes. Come hither, friend.
    Tell me what more thou know'st.   *Exeunt.*

IV, iii   *[Enter Kent and a Gentleman.*

Kent. Why the King of France is so suddenly gone back
    know you no reason?
Gentleman. Something he left imperfect in the state, which
    since his coming forth is thought of, which imports to the
5   kingdom so much fear and danger that his personal re-
    turn was most required and necessary.
Kent. Who hath he left behind him general?
Gentleman. The Marshal of France, Monsieur La Far.
Kent. Did your letters pierce the Queen to any demonstra-
10   tion of grief?
Gentleman. Ay, sir. She took them, read them in my pres-
    ence,
    And now and then an ample tear trilled down
    Her delicate cheek. It seemed she was a queen
    Over her passion, who, most rebel-like,
    Sought to be king o'er her.
15 *Kent.*   O, then it movèd her?

IV, iii, 3 *imperfect . . . state* i.e. rift in affairs of state   4 *imports* means
5 *fear* uneasiness   6 *most* most urgently   9 *pierce* goad   12 *trilled* trickled
14 *who* which

Gentleman. Not to a rage. Patience and sorrow strove
   Who should express her goodliest. You have seen
   Sunshine and rain at once — her smiles and tears
   Were like, a better way: those happy smilets
   That played on her ripe lip seem not to know   20
   What guests were in her eyes, which parted thence
   As pearls from diamonds dropped. In brief,
   Sorrow would be a rarity most belovèd,
   If all could so become it.
Kent.   Made she no verbal question?
Gentleman. Faith, once or twice she heaved the name of
   father   25
   Pantingly forth, as if it pressed her heart;
   Cried 'Sisters, sisters, shame of ladies, sisters!
   Kent, father, sisters? What, i' th' storm i' th' night?
   Let pity not be believed!' There she shook
   The holy water from her heavenly eyes,   30
   And clamor moistened; then away she started
   To deal with grief alone.
Kent.   It is the stars,
   The stars above us govern our conditions;
   Else one self mate and make could not beget
   Such different issues. You spoke not with her since?   35
Gentleman. No.
Kent. Was this before the King returned?
Gentleman.   No, since.
Kent. Well, sir, the poor distressèd Lear's i' th' town;
   Who sometime, in his better tune, remembers

---

17 *goodliest* i.e. most becomingly   19 *Were . . . way* i.e. improved upon
that spectacle   23 *rarity* gem   25–26 *heaved . . . forth* uttered . . . chokingly
29 *Let pity* let it for pity (?)   31 *clamor moistened* i.e. mixed, and thus
muted, lamentation with tears   33 *govern our conditions* determine our
characters   34 *Else . . . make* otherwise the same husband and wife   35 *issues* children   39 *better tune* i.e. more rational state, less jangled

40 What we are come about, and by no means
    Will yield to see his daughter.
    Gentleman.   Why, good sir?
    Kent. A sovereign shame so elbows him; his own unkind-
        ness,
    That stripped her from his benediction, turned her
    To foreign casualties, gave her dear rights
45 To his dog-hearted daughters – these things sting
    His mind so venomously that burning shame
    Detains him from Cordelia.
    Gentleman.   Alack, poor gentleman.
    Kent. Of Albany's and Cornwall's powers you heard not?
    Gentleman. 'Tis so; they are afoot.
50 *Kent.* Well, sir, I'll bring you to our master Lear
    And leave you to attend him. Some dear cause
    Will in concealment wrap me up awhile.
    When I am known aright, you shall not grieve
    Lending me this acquaintance. I pray you go
55 Along with me.   *Exeunt.*]

IV, iv   *Enter, with Drum and Colors, Cordelia, Gentleman [Doc-
         tor], and Soldiers.*

    Cordelia. Alack, 'tis he! Why, he was met even now
    As mad as the vexed sea, singing aloud,
    Crowned with rank fumiter and furrow weeds,
    With hardocks, hemlock, nettles, cuckoo flow'rs,

42 *sovereign* overruling *elbows* jogs 43 *stripped* cut off (cf. 'disbranch,'
IV, ii, 34) *benediction* blessing 44 *casualties* chances 49 *'Tis so* i.e. I have
to this extent 51 *dear cause* important purpose IV, iv, 3 *fumiter* fumitory
furrow weeds (those that appear after ploughing ?) 4 *hardocks* (variously
identified as burdock, 'hoar dock,' 'harlock,' etc.)

Darnel, and all the idle weeds that grow   5
In our sustaining corn. A century send forth!
Search every acre in the high-grown field
And bring him to our eye. [*Exit an Officer.*] What can
   man's wisdom
In the restoring his bereavèd sense?
He that helps him take all my outward worth.   10
Doctor. There is means, madam.
   Our foster nurse of nature is repose,
   The which he lacks. That to provoke in him
   Are many simples operative, whose power
   Will close the eye of anguish.
Cordelia.   All blest secrets,   15
   All you unpublished virtues of the earth,
   Spring with my tears; be aidant and remediate
   In the good man's distress. Seek, seek for him,
   Lest his ungoverned rage dissolve the life
   That wants the means to lead it.

Enter Messenger.

Messenger.   News, madam.   20
   The British pow'rs are marching hitherward.
Cordelia. 'Tis known before. Our preparation stands
   In expectation of them. O dear father,
   It is thy business that I go about.
   Therefore great France   25
   My mourning, and importuned tears hath pitied.

5 *Darnel* tares *idle* useless 6 *sustaining corn* life-giving wheat *century*
troop of a hundred men 8 *can* i.e. can accomplish 9 *bereaved* bereft
10 *outward worth* material possessions 12 *foster* fostering 13 *provoke*
induce 14 *simples operative* medicinal herbs, sedatives 16 *unpublished
virtues* i.e. little-known benign herbs 17 *Spring* grow *remediate* remedial
20 *wants* lacks *means* i.e. power of reason *lead it* govern it (the rage)
25 *Therefore* therefor, because of that 26 *importuned* importunate

No blown ambition doth our arms incite,
But love, dear love, and our aged father's right.
Soon may I hear and see him!   *Exeunt.*

IV, v   *Enter Regan and Steward [Oswald].*

Regan. But are my brother's pow'rs set forth?
Oswald.   Ay, madam.
Regan. Himself in person there?
Oswald.   Madam, with much ado.
   Your sister is the better soldier.
Regan. Lord Edmund spake not with your lord at home?
5 *Oswald.* No, madam.
Regan. What might import my sister's letter to him?
Oswald. I know not, lady.
Regan. Faith, he is posted hence on serious matter.
   It was great ignorance, Gloucester's eyes being out,
10   To let him live. Where he arrives he moves
   All hearts against us. Edmund, I think, is gone,
   In pity of his misery, to dispatch
   His nighted life; moreover, to descry
   The strength o' th' enemy.
15 *Oswald.* I must needs after him, madam, with my letter.
Regan. Our troops set forth to-morrow. Stay with us.
   The ways are dangerous.
Oswald.   I may not, madam.
   My lady charged my duty in this business.
Regan. Why should she write to Edmund? Might not you

---

27 *blown* swollen   IV, v, 2 *much ado* great bother   6 *import* bear as its message   8 *is posted* has sped   9 *ignorance* error   13 *nighted* benighted, blinded   18 *charged* strictly ordered

Transport her purposes by word? Belike,   20
Some things — I know not what. I'll love thee much,
Let me unseal the letter.
Oswald.   Madam, I had rather —
Regan. I know your lady does not love her husband,
I am sure of that; and at her late being here
She gave strange eliads and most speaking looks   25
To noble Edmund. I know you are of her bosom.
Oswald. I, madam?
Regan. I speak in understanding — y'are, I know't —
Therefore I do advise you take this note:
My lord is dead; Edmund and I have talked,   30
And more convenient is he for my hand
Than for your lady's. You may gather more.
If you do find him, pray you give him this;
And when your mistress hears thus much from you,
I pray desire her call her wisdom to her.   35
So fare you well.
If you do chance to hear of that blind traitor,
Preferment falls on him that cuts him off.
Oswald. Would I could meet him, madam! I should show
What party I do follow.
Regan.   Fare thee well.   *Exeunt.* 40

20 *Transport her purposes* convey her intentions *Belike* probably 24 *late*
recently 25 *eliads* amorous glances 26 *of her bosom* in her confidence
29 *take this note* note this 31 *convenient* appropriate 32 *gather more* i.e.
draw your own conclusions 33 *this* this word, this reminder 35 *call*
recall 38 *Preferment* advancement

IV, vi   *Enter Gloucester and Edgar.*

Gloucester. When shall I come to th' top of that same hill?
Edgar. You do climb up it now. Look how we labor.
Gloucester. Methinks the ground is even.
Edgar.   Horrible steep.
  Hark, do you hear the sea?
Gloucester.   No, truly.
5 *Edgar.* Why, then, your other senses grow imperfect
  By your eyes' anguish.
Gloucester.   So may it be indeed.
  Methinks thy voice is altered, and thou speak'st
  In better phrase and matter than thou didst.
Edgar. Y'are much deceived. In nothing am I changed
  But in my garments.
10 *Gloucester.*   Methinks y'are better spoken.
Edgar. Come on, sir; here's the place. Stand still. How
    fearful
  And dizzy 'tis to cast one's eyes so low!
  The crows and choughs that wing the midway air
  Show scarce so gross as beetles. Halfway down
15 Hangs one that gathers sampire — dreadful trade;
  Methinks he seems no bigger than his head.
  The fishermen that walk upon the beach
  Appear like mice; and yond tall anchoring bark,
  Diminished to her cock; her cock, a buoy
20 Almost too small for sight. The murmuring surge
  That on th' unnumb'red idle pebble chafes
  Cannot be heard so high. I'll look no more,

IV, vi, 6 *anguish* affliction 13 *choughs* jackdaws *midway* i.e. halfway
down 14 *gross* large 15 *sampire* samphire (aromatic herb used in relishes)
18 *anchoring* anchored 19 *Diminished . . . cock* reduced to the size of her
cockboat 21 *unnumb'red idle pebble* i.e. barren reach of countless pebbles

136

Lest my brain turn, and the deficient sight
Topple down headlong.
Gloucester.   Set me where you stand.
Edgar. Give me your hand. You are now within a foot   25
Of th' extreme verge. For all beneath the moon
Would I not leap upright.
Gloucester.   Let go my hand.
Here, friend, 's another purse; in it a jewel
Well worth a poor man's taking. Fairies and gods
Prosper it with thee. Go thou further off;   30
Bid me farewell, and let me hear thee going.
Edgar. Now fare ye well, good sir.
Gloucester.   With all my heart.
Edgar. [aside] Why I do trifle thus with his despair
Is done to cure it.
Gloucester.   O you mighty gods!   [He kneels.]
This world I do renounce, and in your sights   35
Shake patiently my great affliction off.
If I could bear it longer and not fall
To quarrel with your great opposeless wills,
My snuff and loathèd part of nature should
Burn itself out. If Edgar live, O bless him!   40
Now, fellow, fare thee well. [He falls forward and swoons.]
Edgar.   Gone, sir — farewell.
And yet I know not how conceit may rob
The treasury of life when life itself
Yields to the theft. Had he been where he thought,

23 *the deficient sight* i.e. my dizziness 24 *Topple* topple me 27 *upright*
i.e. even upright, let alone forward 29 *Fairies* (the usual wardens of
treasure) 33 *Why . . . trifle* i.e. the reason I toy with ('done' in l. 34 being
redundant) 37–38 *fall . . . with* i.e. rebel against (irreligiously) 38 *opposeless* not to be opposed 39 *My snuff . . . nature* i.e. the guttering and hateful
tag end of my life 42 *conceit* imagination 44 *Yields to* i.e. welcomes

137

45   By this had thought been past. Alive or dead?
Ho you, sir! Friend! Hear you, sir? Speak!
Thus might he pass indeed. Yet he revives.
What are you, sir?

Gloucester.   Away, and let me die.

Edgar. Hadst thou been aught but gossamer, feathers, air,

50   So many fathom down precipitating,
Thou'dst shivered like an egg; but thou dost breathe,
Hast heavy substance, bleed'st not, speak'st, art sound.
Ten masts at each make not the altitude
Which thou hast perpendicularly fell.

55   Thy life 's a miracle. Speak yet again.

Gloucester. But have I fall'n, or no?

Edgar. From the dread summit of this chalky bourn.
Look up a-height. The shrill-gorged lark so far
Cannot be seen or heard. Do but look up.

60 *Gloucester.* Alack, I have no eyes.
Is wretchedness deprived that benefit
To end itself by death? 'Twas yet some comfort
When misery could beguile the tyrant's rage
And frustrate his proud will.

Edgar.   Give me your arm.

65   Up – so. How is't? Feel you your legs? You stand.

Gloucester. Too well, too well.

Edgar.   This is above all strangeness.
Upon the crown o' th' cliff what thing was that
Which parted from you?

Gloucester.   A poor unfortunate beggar.

Edgar. As I stood here below, methought his eyes

70   Were two full moons; he had a thousand noses,

---

50 *precipitating* falling   53 *at each* end to end   55 *life* survival   57 *bourn*
boundary, headland   58 *a-height* on high   *gorged* throated   63 *beguile*
outwit   65 *Feel* test

Horns whelked and waved like the enridgèd sea.
It was some fiend. Therefore, thou happy father,
Think that the clearest gods, who make them honors
Of men's impossibilities, have preservèd thee.

Gloucester. I do remember now. Henceforth I'll bear   75
Affliction till it do cry out itself
'Enough, enough, and die.' That thing you speak of,
I took it for a man. Often 'twould say
'The fiend, the fiend' — he led me to that place.

Edgar. Bear free and patient thoughts.

Enter Lear [mad, bedecked with weeds].

                                   But who comes here? 80
The safer sense will ne'er accommodate
His master thus.

Lear. No, they cannot touch me for coining;
I am the King himself.

Edgar. O thou side-piercing sight!   85

Lear. Nature's above art in that respect. There's your press
money. That fellow handles his bow like a crow-keeper.
Draw me a clothier's yard. Look, look, a mouse! Peace,
peace; this piece of toasted cheese will do't. There's my
gauntlet; I'll prove it on a giant. Bring up the brown bills. 90

71 *whelked* corrugated *enridgèd* blown into ridges 72 *happy father* lucky
old man 73 *clearest* purest 73–74 *who . . . impossibilities* i.e. whose glory
it is to do for man what he cannot do for himself 80 *free* (of despair)
81 *safer* saner *accommodate* accoutre 82 *His* its 83 *touch* i.e. interfere with
coining minting coins (a royal prerogative) 86 *Nature . . . respect* i.e. a born
king is above a made king in legal immunity (cf. the coeval debate on the
relative merits of poets of nature, i.e. born, and poets of art, i.e. made by
self-effort) 86–87 *press money* i.e. the 'king's shilling' (token payment on
military impressment or enlistment) 87 *crow-keeper* i.e. farmhand ward-
ing off crows 88 *clothier's yard* i.e. arrow (normally a yard long) 90
gauntlet armored glove (hurled as challenge) *prove it on* maintain it against
brown bills varnished halberds

O, well flown, bird. I' th' clout, i' th' clout – hewgh!
Give the word.
Edgar. Sweet marjoram.
Lear. Pass.
95 *Gloucester.* I know that voice.
Lear. Ha! Goneril with a white beard? They flattered me
like a dog, and told me I had the white hairs in my beard
ere the black ones were there. To say 'ay' and 'no' to
everything that I said! 'Ay' and 'no' too was no good di-
100 vinity. When the rain came to wet me once, and the wind
to make me chatter; when the thunder would not peace
at my bidding; there I found 'em, there I smelt 'em out.
Go to, they are not men o' their words. They told me I
was everything. 'Tis a lie – I am not ague-proof.
105 *Gloucester.* The trick of that voice I do well remember.
Is't not the King?
Lear.　　　　　　Ay, every inch a king.
When I do stare, see how the subject quakes.
I pardon that man's life. What was thy cause?
Adultery?
110 Thou shalt not die. Die for adultery? No.
The wren goes to't, and the small gilded fly
Does lecher in my sight.
Let copulation thrive; for Gloucester's bastard son
Was kinder to his father than my daughters
115 Got 'tween the lawful sheets.

---

91 *well flown* (hawking cry) *clout* bull's-eye (archery term) 92 *word*
password 93 *Sweet marjoram* (herb, associated with treating madness?)
97 *like a dog* i.e. fawningly *I . . . beard* i.e. I was wise 98 *To say . . . 'no'*
i.e. to agree 99–100 *no good divinity* i.e. bad theology (For 'good divinity'
cf. 2 Corinthians 1:18: 'But as God is true, our word to you was not yea
and nay'; also Matthew 5:36–37, James 5:12.) 104 *ague-proof* proof
against chills and fever 105 *trick* peculiarity 108 *cause* case 112 *lecher*
copulate 115 *Got* begotten

To't, luxury, pell-mell, for I lack soldiers.
Behold yond simp'ring dame,
Whose face between her forks presages snow,
That minces virtue, and does shake the head
To hear of pleasure's name.   120
The fitchew nor the soilèd horse goes to't
With a more riotous appetite.
Down from the waist they are Centaurs,
Though women all above.
But to the girdle do the gods inherit,   125
Beneath is all the fiend's.
There's hell, there's darkness, there is the sulphurous pit;
burning, scalding, stench, consumption. Fie, fie, fie! pah,
pah! Give me an ounce of civet; good apothecary, sweeten
my imagination! There's money for thee.   130

Gloucester. O, let me kiss that hand.

Lear. Let me wipe it first; it smells of mortality.

Gloucester. O ruined piece of nature; this great world
  Shall so wear out to naught. Dost thou know me?

Lear. I remember thine eyes well enough. Dost thou squiny 135
  at me? No, do thy worst, blind Cupid; I'll not love.
  Read thou this challenge; mark but the penning of it.

Gloucester. Were all thy letters suns, I could not see.

Edgar. [aside] I would not take this from report — it is,
  And my heart breaks at it.   140

Lear. Read.

116 *luxury* lechery *for . . . soldiers* (and therefore a higher birth rate)
118 *whose . . . snow* i.e. who presents the signs of being sexually cold (*between her forks*, i.e. legs, modifies *snow*) 119 *minces* mincingly affects 120
pleasure's name i.e. the very name of sexual indulgence 121 *fitchew* pole-
cat, prostitute *soilèd* pastured 123 *Centaurs* (lustful creatures of mythology, half-human and half-beast) 125 *girdle* waist *inherit* possess 129 *civet*
musk perfume 132 *mortality* death 133–34 *this . . . naught* i.e. the universe (macrocosm) will decay like this man (microcosm; cf. III, i, 10)
139 *take* accept

Gloucester. What, with the case of eyes?

Lear. O, ho, are you there with me? No eyes in your head,
nor no money in your purse? Your eyes are in a heavy
145 case, your purse in a light; yet you see how this world
goes.

Gloucester. I see it feelingly.

Lear. What, art mad? A man may see how this world goes
with no eyes. Look with thine ears. See how yond justice
150 rails upon yond simple thief. Hark in thine ear. Change
places and, handy-dandy, which is the justice, which is the
thief? Thou hast seen a farmer's dog bark at a beggar?

Gloucester. Ay, sir.

Lear. And the creature run from the cur. There thou
155 mightst behold the great image of authority – a dog's
obeyed in office.
Thou rascal beadle, hold thy bloody hand!
Why dost thou lash that whore? Strip thy own back.
Thou hotly lusts to use her in that kind
160 For which thou whip'st her. The usurer hangs the cozener.
Through tattered clothes small vices do appear;
Robes and furred gowns hide all. Plate sin with gold,
And the strong lance of justice hurtless breaks;
Arm it in rags, a pygmy's straw does pierce it.
165 None does offend, none – I say none! I'll able 'em.

---

142 *case* sockets 143 *are . . . me* is that the situation 145 *case* plight (pun)
147 *feelingly* (1) only by touch (2) by feeling pain 150 *simple* mere
151 *handy-dandy* (old formula used in the child's game of choosing which
hand) 155 *great image* universal symbol 155–56 *a dog's . . . office* i.e. man
bows to authority regardless of who exercises it 157 *beadle* parish con-
stable 159 *lusts* wish (suggestive form of 'lists') *kind* i.e. same act 160
The usurer . . . cozener i.e. the great cheat, some money-lending judge,
sentences to death the little cheat 161 *appear* show plainly 163 *hurtless*
without hurting 164 *Arm . . . rags* i.e. armored (cf. 'Plate,' l. 162) only in
rags 165 *able* authorize

Take that of me, my friend, who have the power
To seal th' accuser's lips. Get thee glass eyes
And, like a scurvy politician, seem
To see the things thou dost not. Now, now, now, now!
Pull off my boots. Harder, harder! So.   170
Edgar. O, matter and impertinency mixed;
Reason in madness.
Lear. If thou wilt weep my fortunes, take my eyes.
I know thee well enough; thy name is Gloucester.
Thou must be patient. We came crying hither;   175
Thou know'st, the first time that we smell the air
We wawl and cry. I will preach to thee. Mark.
Gloucester. Alack, alack the day.
Lear. When we are born, we cry that we are come
To this great stage of fools. — This' a good block.   180
It were a delicate stratagem to shoe
A troop of horse with felt. I'll put't in proof,
And when I have stol'n upon these son-in-laws,
Then kill, kill, kill, kill, kill, kill!

Enter a Gentleman [with Attendants].

Gentleman. O, here he is! Lay hand upon him. — Sir,   185
Your most dear daughter —
Lear. No rescue? What, a prisoner? I am even
The natural fool of fortune. Use me well;
You shall have ransom. Let me have surgeons;
I am cut to th' brains.
Gentleman.   You shall have anything.   190
Lear. No seconds? All myself?

---

166 *that* (i.e. the assurance of immunity) 168 *scurvy politician* vile oppor-
tunist 171 *matter and impertinency* sense and nonsense 180 *block* felt hat (?)
181 *delicate* subtle 182 *in proof* to the test 188 *natural fool* born plaything
190 *cut* wounded

Why, this would make a man a man of salt,
To use his eyes for garden waterpots,
[Ay, and laying autumn's dust.] I will die bravely,
195 Like a smug bridegroom. What, I will be jovial!
Come, come, I am a king; masters, know you that?

Gentleman. You are a royal one, and we obey you.

Lear. Then there's life in't. Come, an you get it, you shall
get it by running. Sa, sa, sa, sa!

Exit [running, followed by Attendants].

200 *Gentleman.* A sight most pitiful in the meanest wretch,
Past speaking of in a king. Thou hast one daughter
Who redeems nature from the general curse
Which twain have brought her to.

Edgar. Hail, gentle sir.

Gentleman.   Sir, speed you. What's your will?

205 *Edgar.* Do you hear aught, sir, of a battle toward?

Gentleman. Most sure and vulgar. Every one hears that
Which can distinguish sound.

Edgar.   But, by your favor,
How near's the other army?

Gentleman. Near and on speedy foot. The main descry
Stands on the hourly thought.

210 *Edgar.*   I thank you, sir. That's all.

Gentleman. Though that the Queen on special cause is here,
Her army is moved on.

Edgar.   I thank you, sir. *Exit [Gentleman].*

Gloucester. You ever-gentle gods, take my breath from me;

192 *salt* i.e. all tears 195 *smug bridegroom* spruce bridegroom (the image
suggested by the secondary meaning of 'bravely,' i.e. handsomely, and the
sexual suggestion of 'will die') 198 *life* (and therefore 'hope') 199 *Sa . . .
sa* (hunting and rallying cry) 202 *general curse* universal condemnation
203 *twain* i.e. the other two 204 *speed* God speed 205 *toward* impending
206 *sure and vulgar* commonly known certainty 209 *on speedy foot* rapidly
marching 209–10 *main . . . thought* sight of the main body is expected
hourly

Let not my worser spirit tempt me again
To die before you please.
Edgar.   Well pray you, father.   215
Gloucester. Now, good sir, what are you?
Edgar. A most poor man, made tame to fortune's blows,
   Who, by the art of known and feeling sorrows,
   Am pregnant to good pity. Give me your hand;
   I'll lead you to some biding.
Gloucester.   Hearty thanks.   220
   The bounty and the benison of heaven
   To boot, and boot.

Enter Steward [Oswald].

Oswald.   A proclaimed prize! Most happy;
   That eyeless head of thine was first framed flesh
   To raise my fortunes. Thou old unhappy traitor,
   Briefly thyself remember. The sword is out   225
   That must destroy thee.
Gloucester.   Now let thy friendly hand
   Put strength enough to't.   *[Edgar interposes.]*
Oswald.   Wherefore, bold peasant,
   Dar'st thou support a published traitor? Hence,
   Lest that th' infection of his fortune take
   Like hold on thee. Let go his arm.   230
Edgar. Chill not let go, zir, without vurther 'casion.
Oswald. Let go, slave, or thou diest.
Edgar. Good gentleman, go your gait, and let poor voke

214 *worser spirit* i.e. bad angel   217 *tame* submissive   218 *art . . . sorrows*
i.e. lesson of sorrows painfully experienced   219 *pregnant* prone   220 *biding* biding place   221 *benison* blessing   222 *proclaimed prize* i.e. one with a
price on his head   *happy* lucky   223 *framed flesh* born, created   225 *thyself
remember* i.e. pray, think of your soul   226 *friendly* i.e. unconsciously be-
friending   228 *published* proclaimed   231 *Chill* I'll (rustic dialect)   *vurther
'casion* further occasion   233 *gait* way   *voke* folk

pass. An chud ha' bin zwaggered out of my life, 'twould
235 not ha' bin zo long as 'tis by a vortnight. Nay, come not
near th' old man. Keep out, che vore ye, or Ise try
whether your costard or my ballow be the harder. Chill
be plain with you.

Oswald. Out, dunghill!   *[They fight.]*

240 *Edgar.* Chill pick your teeth, zir. Come. No matter vor
your foins.   *[Oswald falls.]*

Oswald. Slave, thou hast slain me. Villain, take my
purse.
If ever thou wilt thrive, bury my body,
And give the letters which thou find'st about me
245 To Edmund Earl of Gloucester. Seek him out
Upon the English party. O, untimely death!
Death!   *[He dies.]*

Edgar. I know thee well. A serviceable villain,
As duteous to the vices of thy mistress
As badness would desire.

250 *Gloucester.*   What, is he dead?

Edgar. Sit you down, father; rest you.
Let's see these pockets; the letters that he speaks of
May be my friends. He's dead; I am only sorry
He had no other deathsman. Let us see.
255 Leave, gentle wax; and, manners, blame us not
To know our enemies' minds. We rip their hearts;
Their papers is more lawful.   *Reads the letter.*

---

234 *An chud* if I could *zwaggered* swaggered, bluffed 236 *che vore* I warrant, assure *Ise* I shall 237 *costard* head *ballow* cudgel 240 *Chill pick* i.e.
I'll knock out 241 *foins* thrusts 242 *Villain* serf 244 *letters* letter *about*
upon 246 *party* side 248 *serviceable* usable 249 *duteous* ready to serve
254 *deathsman* executioner 255 *Leave, gentle wax* by your leave, kind
seal (formula used in opening sealed documents) 256 *To know* i.e. for
growing intimate with 257 *Their papers* i.e. to rip their papers

'Let our reciprocal vows be remembered. You have many
opportunities to cut him off. If your will want not, time
and place will be fruitfully offered. There is nothing 260
done, if he return the conqueror. Then am I the prisoner,
and his bed my gaol; from the loathed warmth whereof
deliver me, and supply the place for your labor.
    'Your (wife, so I would say) affectionate servant,
                                         'GONERIL.' 265

O indistinguished space of woman's will —
A plot upon her virtuous husband's life,
And the exchange my brother! Here in the sands
Thee I'll rake up, the post unsanctified
Of murderous lechers; and in the mature time   270
With this ungracious paper strike the sight
Of the death-practiced Duke. For him 'tis well
That of thy death and business I can tell.
Gloucester. The King is mad. How stiff is my vile sense,
That I stand up, and have ingenious feeling   275
Of my huge sorrows! Better I were distract;
So should my thoughts be severed from my griefs,
And woes by wrong imaginations lose
The knowledge of themselves.   *Drum afar off.*
Edgar.   Give me your hand.
Far off methinks I hear the beaten drum.   280
Come, father, I'll bestow you with a friend.   *Exeunt.*

259 *want not* is not lacking   262 *gaol* jail   264 *would* wish to   266 *indistinguished* unlimited   *will* desire   268 *exchange* substitute   269 *rake up*
cover, bury   270 *in the mature* at the ripe   271 *strike* blast   272 *death-
practiced* whose death is plotted   274 *stiff* obstinate   *vile sense* i.e. hateful
consciousness   275 *ingenious feeling* i.e. awareness   276 *distract* distracted
278 *wrong imaginations* i.e. delusions   281 *bestow* lodge

Enter Cordelia, Kent, [Doctor,] and Gentleman.

Cordelia. O thou good Kent, how shall I live and
     work
   To match thy goodness? My life will be too short
   And every measure fail me.
Kent. To be acknowledged, madam, is o'erpaid.
5   All my reports go with the modest truth;
   Nor more nor clipped, but so.
Cordelia.   Be better suited.
   These weeds are memories of those worser hours.
   I prithee put them off.
Kent.   Pardon, dear madam.
   Yet to be known shortens my made intent.
10   My boon I make it that you know me not
   Till time and I think meet.
Cordelia. Then be't so, my good lord. *[to the Doctor]* How
     does the King?
Doctor. Madam, sleeps still.
Cordelia. O you kind gods,
15   Cure this great breach in his abusèd nature!
   Th' untuned and jarring senses, O, wind up
   Of this child-changèd father!
Doctor.   So please your Majesty
   That we may wake the King? He hath slept long.
Cordelia. Be governed by your knowledge, and proceed
20   I' th' sway of your own will. Is he arrayed?

IV, vii, 5 *go* conform 6 *clipped* i.e. less (curtailed) *suited* attired 7 *weeds*
clothes *memories* reminders. 9 *Yet . . . intent* i.e. to reveal myself just yet
would mar my plan 10 *My boon . . . it* the reward I ask is 11 *meet* proper
15 *abusèd* confused, disturbed 16 *jarring* discordant *wind up* tune
17 *child-changèd* (1) changed to a child (2) changed by his children (suggesting 'changeling,' wherein mental defect is associated with the malig-
nance of witches) 20 *I' th' sway of* according to

Enter Lear in a chair carried by Servants.

Gentleman. Ay, madam. In the heaviness of sleep
  We put fresh garments on him.
Doctor. Be by, good madam, when we do awake him.
  I doubt not of his temperance.
[*Cordelia.*   Very well.   [*Music.*]
Doctor. Please you draw near. Louder the music there.]   25
Cordelia. O my dear father, restoration hang
  Thy medicine on my lips, and let this kiss
  Repair those violent harms that my two sisters
  Have in thy reverence made.
Kent.   Kind and dear princess.
Cordelia. Had you not been their father, these white flakes 30
  Did challenge pity of them. Was this a face
  To be opposed against the jarring winds?
  [To stand against the deep dread-bolted thunder?
  In the most terrible and nimble stroke
  Of quick cross lightning to watch, poor perdu,   35
  With this thin helm?] Mine enemy's dog,
  Though he had bit me, should have stood that night
  Against my fire; and wast thou fain, poor father,
  To hovel thee with swine and rogues forlorn
  In short and musty straw? Alack, alack,   40
  'Tis wonder that thy life and wits at once
  Had not concluded all. — He wakes. Speak to him.
Doctor. Madam, do you; 'tis fittest.
Cordelia. How does my royal lord? How fares your
    Majesty?

28 *harms* wounds 29 *reverence* reverend person 30 *flakes* strands of hair
31 *challenge* demand 33 *deep dread-bolted* deep-voiced and full of dreadful
bolts 35 *perdu* (1) expendable outpost (military term) (2) lost one 36 *helm*
military helmet; here, thin hair 38 *fain* glad 40 *short* scanty (?) tramped
to fragments (?)

45 *Lear.* You do me wrong to take me out o' th' grave.
    Thou art a soul in bliss; but I am bound
    Upon a wheel of fire, that mine own tears
    Do scald like molten lead.
    Cordelia.   Sir, do you know me?
    Lear. You are a spirit, I know. Where did you die?
50 *Cordelia.* Still, still, far wide!
    Doctor. He's scarce awake. Let him alone awhile.
    Lear. Where have I been? Where am I? Fair daylight?
    I am mightily abused. I should e'en die with pity
    To see another thus. I know not what to say.
55 I will not swear these are my hands. Let's see –
    I feel this pin prick. Would I were assured
    Of my condition.
    Cordelia.   O look upon me, sir,
    And hold your hand in benediction o'er me.
    You must not kneel.
    Lear.   Pray, do not mock me.
60 I am a very foolish fond old man,
    Fourscore and upward, not an hour more nor less;
    And, to deal plainly,
    I fear I am not in my perfect mind.
    Methinks I should know you, and know this man;
65 Yet I am doubtful, for I am mainly ignorant
    What place this is; and all the skill I have
    Remembers not these garments; nor I know not
    Where I did lodge last night. Do not laugh at me;
    For, as I am a man, I think this lady
    To be my child Cordelia.

47 *wheel of fire* (implement combining the tortures of breaking and burning, figuring in medieval visions of hell) 50 *wide* off the mark 53 *abused* confused

Cordelia.   And so I am! I am!   70
Lear. Be your tears wet? Yes, faith. I pray weep not.
   If you have poison for me, I will drink it.
   I know you do not love me; for your sisters
   Have, as I do remember, done me wrong.
   You have some cause, they have not.
Cordelia.   No cause, no cause. 75
Lear. Am I in France?
Kent.   In your own kingdom, sir.
Lear. Do not abuse me.
Doctor. Be comforted, good madam. The great rage
   You see is killed in him; [and yet it is danger
   To make him even o'er the time he has lost.]   80
   Desire him to go in. Trouble him no more
   Till further settling.
Cordelia. Will't please your Highness walk?
Lear.   You must bear with me.
   Pray you now, forget and forgive. I am old and foolish.
                    Exeunt. [Manent Kent and Gentleman.]
[*Gentleman.* Holds it true, sir, that the Duke of Cornwall 85
   was so slain?
Kent. Most certain, sir.
Gentleman. Who is conductor of his people?
Kent. As 'tis said, the bastard son of Gloucester.
Gentleman. They say Edgar, his banished son, is with the 90
   Earl of Kent in Germany.
Kent. Report is changeable. 'Tis time to look about; the
   powers of the kingdom approach apace.
Gentleman. The arbitrement is like to be bloody. Fare you
   well, sir.   [*Exit.*] 95

---

77 *abuse* deceive   80 *even o'er* fill in   82 *settling* calming   93 *powers*
armies   94 *arbitrement* decisive action

Kent. My point and period will be throughly wrought,
 Or well or ill, as this day's battle's fought.   *Exit.*]

V, i *Enter, with Drum and Colors, Edmund, Regan, Gentle-*
   man, and Soldiers.

Edmund. Know of the Duke if his last purpose hold,
 Or whether since he is advised by aught
 To change the course. He's full of alteration
 And self-reproving. Bring his constant pleasure.

          [Exit an Officer.]

5 *Regan.* Our sister's man is certainly miscarried.
Edmund. 'Tis to be doubted, madam.
Regan.   Now, sweet lord,
 You know the goodness I intend upon you.
 Tell me, but truly — but then speak the truth —
 Do you not love my sister?
Edmund.   In honored love.
10 *Regan.* But have you never found my brother's way
 To the forfended place?
[*Edmund.*   That thought abuses you.
Regan. I am doubtful that you have been conjunct
 And bosomed with her, as far as we call hers.]

---

96 *My point . . . wrought* i.e. my destiny will be completely worked out
97 *Or either* V, i, S.D. *Drum and Colors* drummer and standard-bearers
1 *Know* learn *last purpose hold* most recent intention (i.e. to fight) holds
good 2 *advised* induced 4 *constant pleasure* firm decision 5 *miscarried*
met with mishap 6 *doubted* feared 7 *goodness I intend* boon I plan to confer 9 *honored* honorable 11 *forfended* forbidden *abuses* deceives 12–13
doubtful . . . hers i.e. fearful you have been intimately linked with her both
in mind and body

Edmund. No, by mine honor, madam.

Regan. I never shall endure her. Dear my lord,   15
Be not familiar with her.

Edmund.   Fear me not.
She and the Duke her husband!

Enter, with Drum and Colors, Albany, Goneril, Soldiers.

[*Goneril.* [*aside*] I had rather lose the battle than that sister
Should loosen him and me.]

Albany. Our very loving sister, well bemet.   20
Sir, this I heard: the King is come to his daughter,
With others whom the rigor of our state
Forced to cry out. [Where I could not be honest,
I never yet was valiant. For this business,
It touches us as France invades our land,   25
Not bolds the King with others, whom I fear
Most just and heavy causes make oppose.

Edmund. Sir, you speak nobly.]

Regan.   Why is this reasoned?

Goneril. Combine together 'gainst the enemy;
For these domestic and particular broils   30
Are not the question here.

Albany.   Let's then determine
With th' ancient of war on our proceeding.

[*Edmund.* I shall attend you presently at your tent.]

Regan. Sister, you'll go with us?

Goneril. No.   35

19 *loosen* separate 20 *bemet* met 22 *rigor* tyranny 23 *honest* honorable
25 *touches us as* concerns me because 26–27 *Not bolds . . . oppose* i.e. but
not because he supports the King and others whose truly great grievances
arouse them to arms 28 *reasoned* argued 30 *particular broils* private
quarrels 31 *question* issue 32 *th' ancient of war* i.e. seasoned officers
33 *presently* immediately

Regan. 'Tis most convenient. Pray go with us.
Goneril. O ho, I know the riddle. — I will go.
                                        Exeunt both the Armies.

Enter Edgar.

Edgar. [to Albany] If e'er your Grace had speech with man
    so poor,
  Hear me one word.
Albany.   *[to those departing]* I'll overtake you.
  [to Edgar] Speak.
40 *Edgar.* Before you fight the battle, ope this letter.
  If you have victory, let the trumpet sound
  For him that brought it. Wretched though I seem,
  I can produce a champion that will prove
  What is avouchèd there. If you miscarry,
45   Your business of the world hath so an end,
  And machination ceases. Fortune love you.
Albany. Stay till I have read the letter.
Edgar.   I was forbid it.
  When time shall serve, let but the herald cry,
  And I'll appear again.
50 *Albany.* Why, fare thee well. I will o'erlook thy paper.
                                        Exit [Edgar].

Enter Edmund.

Edmund. The enemy's in view; draw up your powers.
  Here is the guess of their true strength and forces

36 *convenient* fitting *with us* (i.e. with her rather than Edmund as each
leads an 'army' from the stage) 37 *riddle* (i.e. the reason for Regan's
strange demand) 38 *had speech* i.e. has condescended to speak 41 *sound*
sound a summons 43 *prove* (in trial by combat) 44 *avouchèd* charged
46 *machination* i.e. all plots and counterplots 50 *o'erlook* look over
51 *powers* troops 52 *guess* estimate

By diligent discovery; but your haste
Is now urged on you.

Albany.   We will greet the time.   *Exit.*

Edmund. To both these sisters have I sworn my love;   55
  Each jealous of the other, as the stung
  Are of the adder. Which of them shall I take?
  Both? One? Or neither? Neither can be enjoyed,
  If both remain alive. To take the widow
  Exasperates, makes mad her sister Goneril;   60
  And hardly shall I carry out my side,
  Her husband being alive. Now then, we'll use
  His countenance for the battle, which being done,
  Let her who would be rid of him devise
  His speedy taking off. As for the mercy   65
  Which he intends to Lear and to Cordelia —
  The battle done, and they within our power,
  Shall never see his pardon; for my state
  Stands on me to defend, not to debate.   *Exit.*

*Alarum within. Enter, with Drum and Colors, Lear [held   V, ii
  by the hand by] Cordelia; and Soldiers [of France], over
  the stage and exeunt.*

Enter Edgar and Gloucester.

Edgar. Here, father, take the shadow of this tree
  For your good host. Pray that the right may thrive.

53 *discovery* reconnoitering 54 *greet* i.e. meet the demands of 56 *jealous* suspicious 61 *hardly . . . side* with difficulty shall I play my part (as Goneril's lover, or as a great power in England?) 63 *countenance* backing 68–69 *my state . . . debate* i.e. my status depends upon my strength, not my arguments

If ever I return to you again,
I'll bring you comfort.
Gloucester.   Grace go with you, sir.

Exit [Edgar].

Alarum and retreat within. Enter Edgar.

5 *Edgar.* Away, old man! Give me thy hand. Away!
   King Lear hath lost, he and his daughter ta'en.
   Give me thy hand. Come on.
   Gloucester. No further, sir. A man may rot even here.
   Edgar. What, in ill thoughts again? Men must endure
10 Their going hence, even as their coming hither;
   Ripeness is all. Come on.
   Gloucester.   And that's true too.   *Exeunt.*

V, iii   *Enter, in conquest, with Drum and Colors, Edmund; Lear
          and Cordelia as prisoners; Soldiers, Captain.*

   Edmund. Some officers take them away. Good guard
   Until their greater pleasures first be known
   That are to censure them.
   Cordelia.   We are not the first
   Who with best meaning have incurred the worst.
5 For thee, oppressèd king, I am cast down;
   Myself could else outfrown false Fortune's frown.
   Shall we not see these daughters and these sisters?
   Lear. No, no, no, no! Come, let's away to prison.
   We two alone will sing like birds i' th' cage.

V, ii, 4 s.d. *Alarum and retreat* (trumpet sounds, signalling the beginning
and the ending of a battle) 6 *ta'en* captured 8 *rot* i.e. die 9 *ill* i.e.
suicidal *endure* put up with, suffer through 11 *Ripeness* i.e. the time
decreed by the gods for the fruit to fall from the branch V, iii, 2 *greater
pleasures* i.e. the desires of those in higher command 3 *censure* judge
4 *meaning* intentions

When thou dost ask me blessing, I'll kneel down   10
And ask of thee forgiveness. So we'll live,
And pray, and sing, and tell old tales, and laugh
At gilded butterflies, and hear poor rogues
Talk of court news; and we'll talk with them too —
Who loses and who wins; who's in, who's out —   15
And take upon 's the mystery of things
As if we were God's spies; and we'll wear out,
In a walled prison, packs and sects of great ones
That ebb and flow by th' moon.
Edmund.   Take them away.
Lear. Upon such sacrifices, my Cordelia,   20
    The gods themselves throw incense. Have I caught thee?
    He that parts us shall bring a brand from heaven
    And fire us hence like foxes. Wipe thine eyes.
    The goodyears shall devour them, flesh and fell,
    Ere they shall make us weep! We'll see 'em starved first.   25
    Come.   *Exeunt [Lear and Cordelia, guarded].*
Edmund.   Come hither, captain; hark.
    Take thou this note. *[Gives a paper.]* Go follow them to
       prison.
    One step I have advanced thee. If thou dost
    As this instructs thee, thou dost make thy way
    To noble fortunes. Know thou this, that men   30

10–11 *When . . . forgiveness* (cf. IV, vii, 57–59) 12–14 *laugh . . . news* view
with amusement bright ephemera, such as gallants preoccupied with
court gossip 16–17 *take . . . spies* i.e. contemplate the wonder of existence
as if with divine insight, seek eternal rather than temporal truths 17 *wear
out* outlast 18–19 *packs . . . moon* i.e. partisan and intriguing clusters of
'great ones' who gain and lose power monthly 20–21 *Upon . . . incense*
i.e. the gods themselves are the celebrants at such sacrificial offerings to
love as we are 22–23 *He . . . foxes* i.e. to separate us, as foxes are smoked
out and scattered, would require not a human but a heavenly torch
24 *goodyears* (undefined forces of evil) *fell* hide

Are as the time is. To be tender-minded
Does not become a sword. Thy great employment
Will not bear question. Either say thou'lt do't,
Or thrive by other means.
Captain.   I'll do't, my lord.
35 *Edmund.* About it; and write happy when th' hast done.
Mark, I say instantly, and carry it so
As I have set it down.
[*Captain.* I cannot draw a cart, nor eat dried oats —
If it be man's work, I'll do't.]   *Exit.*

Flourish. Enter Albany, Goneril, Regan, Soldiers.

40 *Albany.* Sir, you have showed to-day your valiant strain,
And fortune led you well. You have the captives
Who were the opposites of this day's strife.
I do require them of you, so to use them
As we shall find their merits and our safety
May equally determine.
45 *Edmund.*   Sir, I thought it fit
To send the old and miserable King
To some retention [and appointed guard];
Whose age had charms in it, whose title more,
To pluck the common bosom on his side
50 And turn our impressed lances in our eyes
Which do command them. With him I sent the Queen,
My reason all the same; and they are ready
To-morrow, or at further space, t' appear
Where you shall hold your session. [At this time

31 *as the time is* (i.e. ruthless in war) 32 *become* befit 33 *bear question*
admit discussion 35 *write happy* consider yourself fortunate 42 *opposites of* enemies in 44 *merits* deserts 47 *some . . . guard* detention under
duly appointed guards 49 *pluck . . . bosom* draw popular sympathy
50 *turn . . . eyes* i.e. make our conscripted lancers turn on us 53 *space*
interval 54 *session* trials

We sweat and bleed, the friend hath lost his friend,   55
And the best quarrels, in the heat, are cursed
By those that feel their sharpness.
The question of Cordelia and her father
Requires a fitter place.]
Albany.   Sir, by your patience,
I hold you but a subject of this war,   60
Not as a brother.
Regan.   That's as we list to grace him.
Methinks our pleasure might have been demanded
Ere you had spoke so far. He led our powers,
Bore the commission of my place and person,
The which immediacy may well stand up   65
And call itself your brother.
Goneril.   Not so hot!
In his own grace he doth exalt himself
More than in your addition.
Regan.   In my rights
By me invested, he compeers the best.
Albany. That were the most if he should husband you.   70
Regan. Jesters do oft prove prophets.
Goneril.   Holla, holla!
That eye that told you so looked but asquint.
Regan. Lady, I am not well; else I should answer
From a full-flowing stomach. General,
Take thou my soldiers, prisoners, patrimony;   75
Dispose of them, of me; the walls is thine.

56 *best quarrels* worthiest causes   57 *sharpness* i.e. painful effects   60 *subject of* subordinate in   61 *list to grace* please to honor   65 *immediacy* i.e. present status (as my deputy)   68 *your addition* honors conferred by you   69 *compeers* equals   70 *most* i.e. most complete investiture in your rights *husband* wed   72 *asquint* cross-eyed, crookedly   74 *stomach* anger   75 *patrimony* inheritance.   76 *walls is thine* i.e. you have stormed the citadel (myself)

Witness the world that I create thee here
My lord and master.

Goneril.   Mean you to enjoy him?

Albany. The let-alone lies not in your good will.

Edmund. Nor in thine, lord.

80 *Albany.*   Half-blooded fellow, yes.

Regan. [*to Edmund*] Let the drum strike, and prove my title
      thine.

Albany. Stay yet; hear reason. Edmund, I arrest thee
      On capital treason; and, in thy attaint,
      This gilded serpent. [*Points to Goneril.*] For your claim,
      fair sister,

85   I bar it in the interest of my wife.
      'Tis she is subcontracted to this lord,
      And I, her husband, contradict your banes.
      If you will marry, make your loves to me;
      My lady is bespoke.

Goneril.   An interlude!

90 *Albany.* Thou art armed, Gloucester. Let the trumpet sound.
      If none appear to prove upon thy person
      Thy heinous, manifest, and many treasons,
      There is my pledge. [*Throws down a glove.*] I'll make it on
      thy heart,
      Ere I taste bread, thou art in nothing less
      Than I have here proclaimed thee.

79 *let-alone* permission 80 *Half-blooded* i.e. by birth only half noble
81 *Let . . . thine* i.e. fight and win for yourself my rights in the kingdom
83 *in thy attaint* i.e. as party to your corruption (cf. the 'serpent' of Eden)
86 *subcontracted* i.e. engaged, though previously married (sarcastic play
on 'precontracted,' a legal term applied to one facing an impediment to
marriage because previously engaged to another) 87 *contradict your banes*
forbid your banns, i.e. declare an impediment 88 *loves* love-suits 89 *An
interlude* a quaint playlet (equivalent to saying 'How dramatic!' or 'How
comical!') 93 *make* prove 94 *nothing less* i.e. no respect less guilty

Regan.   Sick, O, sick!   95
Goneril. [aside] If not, I'll ne'er trust medicine.
Edmund. There's my exchange. *[Throws down a glove.]*
    What in the world he is
  That names me traitor, villain-like he lies.
  Call by the trumpet. He that dares approach,
  On him, on you, who not? I will maintain   100
  My truth and honor firmly.
Albany. A herald, ho!
[Edmund.   A herald, ho, a herald!]
Albany. Trust to thy single virtue; for thy soldiers,
  All levied in my name, have in my name
  Took their discharge.
Regan.   My sickness grows upon me.   105
Albany. She is not well. Convey her to my tent.
                              [Exit Regan, attended.]

                Enter a Herald.

  Come hither, herald. Let the trumpet sound,
  And read out this.
[Captain. Sound, trumpet!]   *A trumpet sounds.*
Herald. (reads) 'If any man of quality or degree within the   110
  lists of the army will maintain upon Edmund, supposed
  Earl of Gloucester, that he is a manifold traitor, let him
  appear by the third sound of the trumpet. He is bold in
  his defense.'
[Edmund. Sound!]   *First trumpet.*   115
Herald. Again!   *Second trumpet.*
    Again!   *Third trumpet.*
                              Trumpet answers within.

96 *medicine* i.e. poison   99 *trumpet* trumpeter   103 *single virtue* unaided
prowess   110 *degree* rank   111 *lists* muster

Enter Edgar, armed, [at the third sound, a Trumpet before him].

Albany. Ask him his purposes, why he appears
Upon this call o' th' trumpet.
Herald.   What are you?
120   Your name, your quality, and why you answer
This present summons?
Edgar.   Know my name is lost,
By treason's tooth bare-gnawn and canker-bit;
Yet am I noble as the adversary
I come to cope.
Albany.   Which is that adversary?
Edgar. What's he that speaks for Edmund Earl of Glouces-
125   ter?
Edmund. Himself. What say'st thou to him?
Edgar.   Draw thy sword.
That, if my speech offend a noble heart,
Thy arm may do thee justice. Here is mine.
Behold it is my privilege,
130   The privilege of mine honors,
My oath, and my profession. I protest —
Maugre thy strength, place, youth, and eminence,
Despite thy victor sword and fire-new fortune,
Thy valor and thy heart — thou art a traitor,
135   False to thy gods, thy brother, and thy father,
Conspirant 'gainst this high illustrious prince,
And from th' extremest upward of thy head
To the descent and dust below thy foot

---

122 *canker-bit* eaten, as by the rose-caterpillar 129-31 *it . . . profession* i.e.
wielding this sword is the privilege of my knightly honor, oath, and function 132 *Maugre* in spite of 133 *fire-new* brand-new 134 *heart* courage
136 *Conspirant* in conspiracy 137 *extremest upward* uppermost extreme
138 *descent and dust* i.e. all that intervenes from the head to the dust

A most toad-spotted traitor. Say thou 'no,'
This sword, this arm, and my best spirits are
    bent   140
To prove upon thy heart, whereto I speak,
Thou liest.
Edmund.   In wisdom I should ask thy name,
But since thy outside looks so fair and warlike,
And that thy tongue some say of breeding breathes,
What safe and nicely I might well delay   145
By rule of knighthood I disdain and spurn.
Back do I toss these treasons to thy head,
With the hell-hated lie o'erwhelm thy heart,
Which — for they yet glance by and scarcely bruise —
This sword of mine shall give them instant way   150
Where they shall rest for ever. Trumpets, speak!
                    Alarums. Fight. [Edmund falls.]
Albany. Save him, save him.
Goneril.   This is practice, Gloucester.
By th' law of war thou wast not bound to answer
An unknown opposite. Thou art not vanquished,
But cozened and beguiled.
Albany.   Shut your mouth, dame,   155
Or with this paper shall I stop it. — Hold, sir. —
[To Goneril] Thou worse than any name, read thine own
    evil.
No tearing, lady! I perceive you know it.

139 *toad-spotted* i.e. exuding venom like a toad   140 *bent* directed   142 *wisdom* prudence   144 *some say* some assay, i.e. proof (?) or, one might say (?)
145 *safe and nicely* cautiously and punctiliously   147 *treasons* accusations of treason   148 *hell-hated* hateful as hell   149–51 *Which . . . ever* i.e. the accusations of treason, now flying about harmlessly, will be routed into you with my sword-thrust and lodge there permanently   152 *Save him* spare him (cf. l. 156)   *practice* trickery   155 *cozened* cheated   156 *Hold* wait (If addressed to Edmund, this suggests a motive for the 'Save him' of l. 152: i.e. Albany hopes to obtain a confession.)

Goneril. Say if I do — the laws are mine, not thine.
    Who can arraign me for't?
160 *Albany.*   Most monstrous! O,
    Know'st thou this paper?
Goneril.   Ask me not what I know. *Exit.*
Albany. Go after her. She's desperate; govern her.
                           [Exit an Officer.]
Edmund. What you have charged me with, that have I done,
    And more, much more. The time will bring it out.
165 'Tis past, and so am I. — But what art thou
    That hast this fortune on me? If thou'rt noble,
    I do forgive thee.
Edgar.   Let's exchange charity.
    I am no less in blood than thou art, Edmund;
    If more, the more th' hast wronged me.
170 My name is Edgar and thy father's son.
    The gods are just, and of our pleasant vices
    Make instruments to plague us.
    The dark and vicious place where thee he got
    Cost him his eyes.
Edmund.   Th' hast spoken right; 'tis true.
175 The wheel is come full circle; I am here.
Albany. Methought thy very gait did prophesy
    A royal nobleness. I must embrace thee.
    Let sorrow split my heart if ever I
    Did hate thee, or thy father.
Edgar.   Worthy prince, I know't.
180 *Albany.* Where have you hid yourself?
    How have you known the miseries of your father?

159 *mine* (i.e. as ruler) 162 *govern* control 166 *fortune on* i.e. victory over 167 *charity* forgiveness and love 169 *If more* if greater (since legitimate) 171 *of our pleasant* out of our pleasurable 173 *place* i.e. the bed of adultery *got* begot 175 *wheel* (of fortune) *here* (at its bottom) 176 *prophesy* promise

Edgar. By nursing them, my lord. List a brief tale;
  And when 'tis told, O that my heart would burst!
  The bloody proclamation to escape
  That followed me so near (O, our lives' sweetness!   185
  That we the pain of death would hourly die
  Rather than die at once) taught me to shift
  Into a madman's rags, t' assume a semblance
  That very dogs disdained; and in this habit
  Met I my father with his bleeding rings,   190
  Their precious stones new lost; became his guide,
  Led him, begged for him, saved him from despair;
  Never – O fault! – revealed myself unto him
  Until some half hour past, when I was armed,
  Not sure, though hoping of this good success,   195
  I asked his blessing, and from first to last
  Told him our pilgrimage. But his flawed heart –
  Alack, too weak the conflict to support –
  'Twixt two extremes of passion, joy and grief,
  Burst smilingly.
Edmund.   This speech of yours hath moved me,   200
  And shall perchance do good; but speak you on –
  You look as you had something more to say.
Albany. If there be more, more woeful, hold it in,
  For I am almost ready to dissolve,
  Hearing of this.
[*Edgar.*   This would have seemed a period   205
  To such as love not sorrow; but another,
  To amplify too much, would make much more,
  And top extremity.

185–86 O . . . *die* i.e. how sweet is life that we would prefer to suffer
death-pangs hourly 189 *habit* attire 190 *rings* sockets 194 *armed* in
armor 197 *our pilgrimage* of our journey *flawed* cracked 204 *dissolve*
melt into tears 205 *a period* the limit 206–8 *another . . . extremity* i.e.
another sorrow, too fully described, would exceed the limit

Whilst I was big in clamor, came there in a man,
210   Who, having seen me in my worst estate,
Shunned my abhorred society; but then, finding
Who 'twas that so endured, with his strong arms
He fastenèd on my neck, and bellowèd out
As he'd burst heaven, threw him on my father,
215   Told the most piteous tale of Lear and him
That ever ear received; which in recounting
His grief grew puissant, and the strings of life
Began to crack. Twice then the trumpets sounded,
And there I left him trancèd.

Albany.   But who was this?

220 *Edgar.* Kent, sir, the banished Kent; who in disguise
Followèd his enemy king and did him service
Improper for a slave.]

Enter a Gentleman [with a bloody knife].

Gentleman. Help, help! O, help!

Edgar.   What kind of help?

Albany.   Speak, man.

Edgar. What means this bloody knife?

Gentleman.   'Tis hot, it smokes.
225   It came even from the heart of — O, she's dead.

Albany. Who dead? Speak, man.

Gentleman. Your lady, sir, your lady; and her sister
By her is poisonèd; she confesses it.

Edmund. I was contracted to them both. All three
Now marry in an instant.

230 *Edgar.*   Here comes Kent.

209 *big in clamor* loud in lamentation   210 *estate* state   **217** *puissant*
powerful   219 *trancèd* insensible   221 *enemy* inimical   **224** *smokes* steams
229 *contracted* engaged   230 *marry* (i.e. in death)

Enter Kent.

Albany. Produce the bodies, be they alive or dead.
                                   [Exit Gentleman.]
  This judgment of the heavens, that makes us tremble,
  Touches us not with pity. — O, is this he?
  The time will not allow the compliment
  Which very manners urges.
Kent.   I am come   235
  To bid my king and master aye good night.
  Is he not here?
Albany.   Great thing of us forgot!
  Speak, Edmund, where's the King? and where's Cordelia?
                  Goneril and Regan's bodies brought out.
  Seest thou this object, Kent?
Kent. Alack, why thus?
Edmund.   Yet Edmund was beloved.   240
  The one the other poisoned for my sake,
  And after slew herself.
Albany. Even so. Cover their faces.
Edmund. I pant for life. Some good I mean to do,
  Despite of mine own nature. Quickly send —   245
  Be brief in it — to the castle, for my writ
  Is on the life of Lear and on Cordelia.
  Nay, send in time.
Albany.   Run, run, O, run!
Edgar. To who, my lord? Who has the office? Send
  Thy token of reprieve.   250

234 *compliment* ceremony 235 *very manners* i.e. sheer decency 237 *thing*
matter *of* by 239 *object* sight 240 *Yet* despite all 244 *pant for life* i.e.
gasp for life's breath 246 *writ* i.e. order of execution 249 *office* commission

Edmund. Well thought on. Take my sword;
 Give it the captain.
Edgar.   Haste thee for thy life. *[Exit Officer.]*
Edmund. He hath commission from thy wife and me
 To hang Cordelia in the prison and
255 To lay the blame upon her own despair
 That she fordid herself.
Albany. The gods defend her! Bear him hence awhile.
           [Edmund is borne off.]

 *Enter Lear, with Cordelia in his arms, [Gentleman, and
  others following].*

Lear. Howl, howl, howl! O, you are men of stones.
 Had I your tongues and eyes, I'd use them so
260 That heaven's vault should crack. She's gone for ever.
 I know when one is dead, and when one lives.
 She's dead as earth. Lend me a looking glass.
 If that her breath will mist or stain the stone,
 Why then she lives.
Kent.   Is this the promised end?
Edgar. Or image of that horror?
265 *Albany.*   Fall and cease.
Lear. This feather stirs; she lives! If it be so,
 It is a chance which does redeem all sorrows
 That ever I have felt.
Kent.   O my good master.
Lear. Prithee away.
Edgar.   'Tis noble Kent, your friend.
270 *Lear.* A plague upon you murderers, traitors all;
 I might have saved her; now she's gone for ever.

256 *fordid* destroyed 263 *stone* i.e. glass 264 *promised end* i.e. doomsday
265 *image* duplicate *Fall and cease* i.e. strike once and for all, make an end
of things 267 *redeem* atone for

Cordelia, Cordelia, stay a little. Ha,
What is't thou say'st? Her voice was ever soft,
Gentle, and low — an excellent thing in woman.
I killed the slave that was a-hanging thee.   275
Gentleman. 'Tis true, my lords, he did.
Lear.   Did I not, fellow?
I have seen the day, with my good biting falchion
I would have made them skip. I am old now,
And these same crosses spoil me. Who are you?
Mine eyes are not o' th' best. I'll tell you straight.   280
Kent. If fortune brag of two she loved and hated,
One of them we behold.
Lear. This is a dull sight. Are you not Kent?
Kent.   The same:
Your servant Kent; where is your servant Caius?
Lear. He's a good fellow, I can tell you that.   285
He'll strike, and quickly too. He's dead and rotten.
Kent. No, my good lord; I am the very man.
Lear. I'll see that straight.
Kent. That from your first of difference and decay
Have followed your sad steps.
Lear.   You are welcome hither.   290
Kent. Nor no man else. All's cheerless, dark, and deadly.
Your eldest daughters have fordone themselves,
And desperately are dead.

---

277 *falchion* small sword slightly hooked   279 *crosses* adversities   *spoil me*
i.e. sap my strength   280 *tell you straight* i.e. recognize you in a moment
281 *two* (i.e. Lear, and a hypothetical second extreme example of Fortune's
cruelty with whom he may be equated)   *loved and hated* i.e. favored, then
victimized   283 *sight* eyesight (Instinctively Lear shuns the admission that
he is dazed and weeping.)   284 *Caius* (Kent's alias)   288 *see that straight*
understand that in a moment   289 *difference and decay* change and decline
in fortune   291 *Nor no man else* i.e. no, nor anyone else   292 *fordone* destroyed   293 *desperately* in a state of despair

Lear.   Ay, so I think.
Albany. He knows not what he says; and vain is it
    That we present us to him.
295 *Edgar.*   Very bootless.

Enter a Messenger.

Messenger. Edmund is dead, my lord.
Albany.   That's but a trifle here.
    You lords and noble friends, know our intent.
    What comfort to this great decay may come
    Shall be applied. For us, we will resign,
300 During the life of this old Majesty,
    To him our absolute power; *[to Edgar and Kent]* you to
        your rights,
    With boot and such addition as your honors
    Have more than merited. All friends shall taste
    The wages of their virtue, and all foes
305 The cup of their deservings. — O, see, see!
Lear. And my poor fool is hanged: no, no, no life?
    Why should a dog, a horse, a rat, have life,
    And thou no breath at all? Thou'lt come no more,
    Never, never, never, never, never.
310 Pray you undo this button. Thank you, sir.
    Do you see this? Look on her! Look her lips,
    Look there, look there —   *He dies.*
Edgar.   He faints. My lord, my lord —
Kent. Break, heart, I prithee break!
Edgar.   Look up, my lord.

295 *bootless* useless 298 *What . . . come* i.e. whatever means of aiding this
ruined great one presents itself 302 *boot* good measure *addition* titles,
advancement in rank 306 *fool* i.e. Cordelia ('Fool' was often a term of
affection, and sometimes, as in Erasmus and elsewhere in Shakespeare,
of praise—as ironic commentary upon self-seeking 'worldly wisdom.')

Kent. Vex not his ghost. O, let him pass! He hates him
   That would upon the rack of this tough world   315
   Stretch him out longer.
Edgar.   He is gone indeed.
Kent. The wonder is, he hath endured so long.
   He but usurped his life.
Albany. Bear them from hence. Our present business
   Is general woe. *[to Kent and Edgar]* Friends of my soul,
      you twain   320
   Rule in this realm, and the gored state sustain.
Kent. I have a journey, sir, shortly to go.
   My master calls me; I must not say no.
Edgar. The weight of this sad time we must obey,
   Speak what we feel, not what we ought to say.   325
   The oldest hath borne most; we that are young
   Shall never see so much, nor live so long.
                          Exeunt with a dead march.

314 *Vex . . . ghost* do not trouble his departing spirit 315 *rack* instrument
of torture 318 *usurped* possessed contrary to (natural) law 324 *obey* i.e.
accept

Appendix: The Quarto Text

The present edition, as explained in the "Note on the text," adheres closely to the folio version of the play. The quarto version, although inferior in the main, is of great literary interest. The essential material for a comparison of the verbal features of the two versions is here supplied.

Mechanically, the quarto text is very defective: stage directions are often lacking and the speakers are confusingly designated; the punctuation is bad; and the verse is often printed as prose, the prose as verse. Omitted from the quarto but included in the folio are passages totalling approximately 100 lines, appearing in the present edition at the following points: I, i, 40–45 *while . . . now* 49–50 *Since . . . state* 64–65 *and . . . rivers* 83–85 *to whose . . . interest* 88–89 *Nothing . . . Nothing* 162 *Dear . . . forbear;* I, ii, 107–11 *This villain . . . graves* 160–65 *I pray . . . brother;* I, iv, 252 *Pray . . . patient* 265 *Of . . . you* 313–24 *This man . . . Oswald;* II, iv, 6 *No . . . lord* 21 *By Juno . . . ay* 45–53 *Winter's . . . year* 93–94 *Well . . . man* 98 *Are . . . blood* 135–40 *Say . . . blame* 291–92 *Whither . . . horse;* III, i, 22–29 *Who have . . . furnishings;* III, ii, 79–96 *This . . . time;* III, iv, 17–18 *In . . . endure* 26–27 *In, boy . . . sleep* 37–38 *Fathom . . . Tom;* III, vi, 12–14 *No . . . him* 83 *And . . . noon;* IV, i, 6–9 *Welcome . . . blasts;* IV, ii, 25 *My . . . Gloucester;* IV, vi, 162–67 *Plate . . . lips;* V, ii, 11 *And . . . too;* V, iii, 76 *Dispose . . . thine* 89 *An interlude* 145 *What . . . delay* 223 *Speak, man* 311–12 *Do . . . there.*

On the other hand, included in the quarto but omitted from the folio are passages totalling approximately 283 lines—inserted in square brackets in the present edition at the following points: I, i, 104; I, ii, 93–95, 140–47; I, iii, 16–20, 24–25; I, iv, 133–48, 222–25, 248, 295; II, i, 78; II, ii, 136–40, 146; II, iv, 18–19; III, i, 7–15, 30–42; III, vi, 17–55, 95–99, 100–13; III, vii, 99–107; IV, i, 58–63; IV, ii, 31–50, 53–59, 62–69; IV, iii, 1–55; IV, vi, 194; IV, vii, 24–25, 33–36, 79–80, 85–97; V, i, 11–13, 18–19, 23–28, 33; V, iii, 38–39, 47, 54–59, 102, 109, 115, 205–22. In addition, the following words in the present edition represent insertions from the quarto: I, i, 214 *best* 289 *not;* I, ii, 127 *Fut* 129 *Edgar* 130 *and* 166 *Go armed;* II, i, 71 *ay;* II, iii, 15 *bare;* III, iv, 127 *had;* IV, vii, 24 *not;* V, i, 16 *me.*

173

The wording of the quarto text differs from that of the folio in hundreds of instances. In the present edition a quarto reading has been substituted for a folio reading only when the latter makes poor or obviously inferior sense. The list of such substitutions follows, with the adopted quarto readings given in italics, the corresponding folio reading in roman:

I, i, 5 *equalities* qualities   74 *possesses* professes   170 *sentence* sentences   188 *Gloucester* Cordelia   206 *on* in   221 *Fall'n* Fall   225 *well* will   248 *respects of fortune* respect and fortunes   302 *hit* sit.

I, iv, 1 *well* will   93 *Kent.* **Why, fool** Lear. Why, my boy   163 *e'er* (from '*euer*') ere   169 *fools* fool   194 *endurèd* endured   334 *atasked* at task.

II, i, 70 *I should* should I   79 *why* where   87 *strange news* strangeness   115 *Natures* Nature's

II, ii, 21 *clamorous* clamors   70 *too t'*   73 *Renege* Revenge   74 *gale* gall   118 *dread* dead   125 *respect* respects

II, iv, 2 *messenger* messengers   30 *panting* painting   33 *whose* those   126 *mother's* mother   181 *fickle* 'fickly'

III, ii, 3 *drowned* drown

III, iv, 52 *ford* sword   86 *deeply* dearly   109 *till the* at   126 *stock-punished* stocked, punished

III, v, 24 *dearer* dear

III, vi, 68 *tike* tight   75 *makes* make

IV, ii, 75 *thereat enraged* threat-enraged   79 *justicers* justices

IV, iv, 18 *distress* desires

IV, vi, 17 *walk* walked   71 *enridgèd* enragèd   83 *coining* crying   161 *small* great   201 *one* a

V, i, 46 *love* loves

V, iii, 83 *attaint* arrest   84 *sister* sisters   97 *he is* he's   160 *Goneril* Bastard (i.e. Edmund)   278 *them* him

Omitted from the above list are a few instances of variation in which a folio misprint would have been detectable without reference to the quarto. Omitted from the following list are numerous instances of slight variation between quarto and folio in the use of articles, prepositions, elision, number, tense, etc., in which the literary interest is small. In all such instances the folio has been followed in the present edition, as well as in the variations listed below. Here the accepted folio readings are given in italics, the corresponding quarto readings in roman. The great majority of the latter are, by common consent, inferior, but while these cast suspicion upon all, the fact remains that a certain number are not inferior to the folio readings and may represent what Shakespeare actually wrote. Marked with stars are the quarto readings which seem to the present editor best able to compete with the folio readings when judged from a purely literary point of view:

I, i, 20 *to* into 34 *the* my 35 *lord* liege 37 *Give me the map there. Know that we have divided* *The map there. Know we have divided 38 *fast* first 39 *from our age* of our state 40 *Conferring* Confirming 40 *strengths* years 45 *The princes* The two great princes 53 *Where nature doth with merit challenge* Where merit doth most challenge it 55 *love* do love 62 *speak* do 64 *shadowy* shady 68 *of Cornwall* *to Cornwall? Speak 69 *of that self mettle as my sister* of the selfsame mettle that my sister is 72 *comes too* came 78 *ponderous* richer 82 *conferred* confirmed 83 *our last and least* the last, not least in our dear love 85 *draw* win 86 *sisters? Speak* sisters 90 *Nothing will* How? Nothing can 94 *How, how, Cordelia* Go to, Go to 95 *you* it 108 *Let* Well, let 118 *shall to my bosom* shall 130 *with* in 135 *shall* still 149 *falls* stoops 149 *Reserve thy state* *Reverse thy doom 156 *ne'er* nor 157 *motive* the motive 161 *Miscreant* Recreant 163 *Kill* Do. Kill 164 *gift* doom 166 *Hear me, recreant* Hear me 168 *That* Since 168 *vows* vow 169 *strained* strayed 173 *Five* Four 174 *disasters* *diseases 175 *sixth* fifth 180 *Fare* Why, fare 181 *Freedom* Friendship 182 *dear shelter* protection 190 *this* a 193 *Most royal* Royal 194 *hath* what 200 *more* else 202 *Will* Sir, will 204 *Dow'red* Covered 214 *whom* that 216 *The best, the dearest* Most best, most dearest 223 *Should* Could 226 *make known* may know 228 *unchaste* *unclean 230 *richer* rich 232

That As 233 *Better* Go to, go to. Better 235 *but* no more but 239 *regards* respects 241 *a dowry* and dower 241 *King* Lear 258 *of* in 259 *Can* Shall 271 *Love* Use 276 *duty* duties 280 *plighted* pleated 281 *with shame* shame them 283 *not little* not a little 291 *grossly* gross 305 *of it* on't

I, ii, 10 *With base? with baseness? Bastardy base? Base* With base, base bastardy 15 *then* the 18 *legitimate. Fine word, 'legitimate'* legitimate 24 *prescribed* subscribed 38 *o'erlooking* liking 45 *policy and reverence* policy 68 *before* heretofore 70 *heard him oft* often heard him 71–72 *declined* declining 76 *sirrah* sir 76 *I'll* I 85 *that he hath writ* he hath wrote 86 *other* further 100 *find* see 102–3 *reason it* reason 118 *on* by 120 *spherical* spiritual 124 *on* to 124 *a star* stars 128–29 *bastardizing* bastardy 130 *pat* out 131 *Tom o'* them of 132–33 *divisions. Fa, sol, la, mi* divisions 138 *with* about 139 *writes* writ 148 *The night* Why, the night 150 *Ay, two* Two

i, iii, 13 *fellows* fellow servants 13 *to* in 14 *distaste* dislike 18 *my* our 21 *have said* tell you 21 *Well* Very well 26 *course* *very course 26 *Prepare* Go prepare

I, iv, 20 *be'st* be 30 *canst thou* canst 43 *You, you* You 68 *my* this 72 *noted it well* noted it 75 *you, sir, you* you sir, you sir 75 *hither, sir* hither 79 *your pardon* you pardon me 81 *strucken* struck 85 *sir, arise, away* sir 87 *Go to! Have you wisdom? So* You have wisdom 97 *did* done 106 *the Lady Brach* Lady o' the Brach 111 *nuncle* uncle 122 *Kent* Lear 123 *'tis like* like 125 *nuncle* uncle 131 *sweet one* sweet fool 158 *grace* wit 160 *And* They 160 *to wear* do wear 172 *lie, sirrah* lie 181 *You* *Methinks you 183 *frowning* *frown 188 *nor crust* neither crust 204 *Will* Must 205 *know* trow 210 *I would* Come, sir, I would 210 *your* that 212 *transport* transform 216 *This* Why, this 219 *Ha! Waking? 'Tis* Sleeping or waking? Ha! Sure 'tis 227 *This admiration, sir* Come, sir, this admiration 229 *To understand* Understand 236 *graced* great 237 *then* thou 248 *Woe* We 248 *repents* repent's 261 *Lear, Lear, Lear* Lear, Lear 266 *Hear* Hark 280 *Away, away* Go, go, my people 282 *more of it* the cause 294 *loose* make 296 *Ha! Let it be so. I have another daughter* *Let it be so. Yet have I left a daughter 301 *ever* ever. Thou shalt, I warrant thee 301 *that* that, my lord 304 *Pray you, content.—*

What, Oswald, ho Come, sir, no more 306 *tarry* tarry and
331 *No, no,* Now 333 *condemn* dislike

I, v, 4 *afore* before 10 *not* ne'er 13–14 *can tell what* can what
15 *What canst tell, boy* Why, what canst thou tell, my boy 17
canst canst not 17 *i' th' middle on's* in the middle of his 31 *moe*
more 33 *Yes indeed* Yes 38 *till* before 40 *O, let me not be mad,
not mad, sweet heaven* O, let me not be mad, sweet heaven. I would
not be mad 42 *How now, are* Are 45 *that's a* that is 46 *unless*
except

II, i, 3–4 *Regan his Duchess* his Duchess 4 *this* to 7 *they* there
8 *ear-kissing* *ear-bussing 10 *the* the two 13 *may do* may 18 *I
must act. Briefness* must ask briefness 18 *work* help 23 *Cornwall*
Cornwall ought 27 *yourself* your— 30 *Draw, seem* Seem 31 *ho*
here 32 *Fly, brother* Fly, brother, fly 39 *Mumbling* Warbling
40 *stand* stand's 43 *him, ho* him 46 *the thunder* *their thunders
52 *latched* lanched 56 *Full* But 62 *coward* caitiff 68 *would the
reposal* could the reposure 73 *practice* pretence 76 *spirits* spurs
77 *O strange* *Strong 78 *letter, said he* letter 90 *O madam*
Madam 90 *it's cracked* *is cracked 97 *he was of that consort* he
was 100 *th' expense and waste* the waste and spoil 120 *prize* poise

II, ii, 1 *dawning* even 5 *lov'st* love 15–16 *action-taking* action-
taking knave. A 16 *superserviceable, finical* superfinical 21
deny'st deny 28 *night, yet* night 29 *You* Draw, you 32 *come
with* bring 39 *Murder, murder* Murder! help 48 *matter?* Part
matter 54 *they* he 54–55 *years o' th' trade* hours at the trade
64 *know you* you have 69 *atwain* in twain 72 *Being* *Bring
72 *the* *their 79 *drive* send 84 *fault* offense 90 *some* a 94 *An
honest mind and plain* He must be plain 100 *faith* sooth 101 *great*
grand 103 *mean'st* mean'st thou 113 *compact* conjunct 120
Fetch Bring 121 *ancient* miscreant 122 *Sir, I* I 127 *Stocking*
Stopping 133 *color* nature 141 *King his master needs must* King
must 142 *he* he's 147 *Cornwall. Come, my lord, away* *Regan.
Come, my good lord, away 152 *out* on't 155 *taken* took

II, iii, 1 *heard* hear 10 *hairs in* hair with 19 *Sometimes* Sometime

II, iv, 3 *purpose in them* purpose 5 *Ha* How 7 *he* look, he
8 *heads* heels 25 *impose* purpose 34 *meiny* men 57 *here* within

within 58 *here* there 59 *but* than 60 *None* no 61 *number* train 68 *twenty* a hundred 70 *following* following it 70–71 *upward* up the hill 74 *which serves and seeks* that serves 83 *stocks, fool* stocks 85 *have travelled all the night* travelled hard to-night 91 *Fiery? What quality* What fiery quality 97 *commands—tends—service* *commands her service 99 *Fiery? The fiery Duke* Fiery Duke 99 *that* that Lear 111 *Go tell* Tell 116 *O me, my heart, my rising heart! But down* O my heart, my heart 118 *knapped* rapped 132 *With* Of 135 *scant* slack 143 *his* *her 148 *you but* you 153 *Never* No 163 *blister* blast her pride 164 *mood is on* *mood— 186 *you yourselves* yourselves 189 *will you* wilt thou 217 *that's in* that lies within 227 *looked* look 230 *you* you are 251 *look* seem 258 *need* needs 267 *man* fellow 272 *And let* O let 293 *best* good 295 *high* *bleak 296 *ruffle* rustle 297 *scarce* not

III, i, s.D. *severally* at several doors 1 *Who's there besides* What's there beside 4 *elements* element 18 *note* art 20 *is* be 48 *that* *your 53–54 *King—in which your pain That way, I'll this* King— I'll this way, you that

III, ii, 7 *Strike* Smite 16 *tax* task 18 *Then* Now then 22 *will* have 22 *join* joined 42 *are* sit 49 *fear* force 50 *pudder* pother 54 *simular* simular man 55 *to* in 58 *concealing continents* concealed centers 64 *harder than the stones* hard than is the stone 71 *And* *That 73 *That's sorry* That sorrows 74 *has and* has 77 *Though* For 78 *boy* my good boy

III, iii, 4 *perpetual* their 12 *footed* landed 13 *look* seek 15 *If I* Though I 17 *strange things* some strange thing 23 *The* Then 23 *doth* do

III, iv, 4 *enter here* enter 6 *contentious* tempestuous 16 *home* sure 22 *enter here* enter 29 *storm* night 46 *blow the winds* *blows the cold wind 46 *Humh! go* Go 46 *bed* *cold bed 48 *Didst thou give all to thy* Hast given all to thy two 54 *porridge* pottage 57 *acold. O, do, de, do, de, do, de* acold 60 *there—and there again— and there* and there again 61 *Has his* What, his 62 *Wouldst* Didst 66 *light* fall 74 *Alow, alow, loo, loo* Alo, lo, lo 77 *words' justice* words justly 94 *says suum, mun* hay 96 *Thou* Why, thou 96 *a* thy 98 *more than* *more but 100 *Ha! here's* here's 104

contented; 'tis content; this is 108 *foul* foul fiend 110 *squints*
*squemes (i.e. squinies?) 132 *Smulkin* Snulbug 148 *same* most
152 *him once more* him 162 *mercy, sir* mercy 173 *tower came*
town come

III, v, 9 *letter which* *letter 11 *this* his

III, vi, 68 *Or bobtail* *Bobtail 69 *him* them 71 *leaped* *leap
72 *Do, de, de, de. Sessa* Loudla doodla 76 *these hard hearts* this
hardness 78 *You will* You'll 78 *Persian* Persian attire 80 *here
and rest* here 82 *So, so. We'll go to supper i' th' morning* So, so,
so. We'll go to supper i' th' morning. So, so, so. 93 *up, take up*
up the King

III, vii, 3 *traitor* villain 23 *Though well* Though 32 *I'm none*
I am true 42 *answered* answerer 53 *answer* first answer 58 *stick*
*rash (meaning 'rip') 59 *bare* lowed 62 *rain* rage 63 *stern*
*dearn (meaning 'drear') 65 *subscribe* *subscribed 73 *served you*
served 79 *Nay* Why 81 *you have* *yet have you 86 *enkindle*
unbridle 87 *treacherous villain* villain

IV, i, 4 *esperance* experience 9 *But who comes* Who's 10 *poorly
led* parti, eyd (sic) 14 *These fourscore years* This fourscore—
17 *You* Alack, sir, you 36 *flies to* flies are to th' 41 *Get thee away*
*Then prithee get thee gone 45 *Which* Who 52 *daub* dance
54 *And yet I must.—Bless* Bless 57–58 *thee, good man's son* the
good man

IV, ii, 17 *names* *arms 28 *My fool* A fool 28 *body* bed 29
whistle whistling 60 *seems* *shows 73 *thrilled* thralled

IV, iv, 10 *helps* can help 26 *importuned* important

IV, v, 15 *him, madam* him 40 *party* Lady

IV, vi, 1 *I* we 8 *In* With 46 *sir! Friend* sir 51 *Thou'dst* Thou
hadst 65 *How is't* How 73 *make them* made their 78 *'twould*
would it 89 *this piece of* this 91 *I' th' clout, i' th' clout* in the air,
hah 96 *Goneril with a white beard* Goneril, ha Regan 104 *ague-
proof* argue-proof 127 *sulphurous* sulphury 128 *consumption*
consummation 129 *sweeten* *to sweeten 132 *Let me* Here
138 *thy* the 138 *see* see one 148 *this* the 150–51 *Change
places and, handy-dandy* Handy-dandy 159 *Thou* Thy blood

161 *clothes* rags   169 *Now, now, now, now* No, now   177 *wawl*
wail   177 *Mark* Mark me   182 *felt. I'll put't in proof* felt   186 *dear
daughter—* dear—   192 *a man a man* a man   195 *smug bridegroom*
bridegroom   198 *Come* Nay   199 *running. Sa, sa, sa, sa* running
207 *sound* sense   217 *tame to* lame by   224 *old* most   237 *ballow*
bat   246 *English* *British   252 *these* his   264 *servant* *servant, and
for you her own for venture (sic)   277 *severed* *fencèd

IV, vii, 16 *jarring* hurrying   32 *opposed* exposed   32 *jarring*
*warring 36 *enemy's* injurious   58 *hand* hands   59 *You* No, sir,
you   59 *mock me* mock   61 *upward, not an hour more nor less*
upward   70 *I am! I am* I am   79 *killed* cured   84 *Pray you* Pray

V, i, 21 *heard* hear   36 *Pray* Pray you   46 *And machination ceases.
Fortune* Fortune   52 *true* great

V, ii, 1 *tree* bush

V, iii, 8 *No, no, no, no* No, no   25 *starved* starve   43 *I* We
62 *might* should   68 *addition* advancement   78 *him* him then
81 *thine* good   90 *Gloucester. Let the trumpet sound* Gloucester
91 *person* head   93 *make* prove   96 *medicine* poison   99 *the* thy
105 *My* This   110 *within the lists* in the host   113 *by* at   120 *name,
your* name and   124 *cope* *cope withal   128–29 *my privilege,
The privilege of mine honors* the privilege of my tongue   136
Conspirant Conspicuate   138 *below thy foot* beneath thy feet
144 *tongue* being   146 *rule* right   147 *Back* Here   152 *practice*
*mere practice   153 *war* *arms   155 *Shut* *Stop   156 *stop*
*stopple   156 *it.—Hold, sir* it   157 *name* thing   172 *plague*
*scourge   174 *right; 'tis true* truth   186 *we* with   191 *Their* The
197 *our* my   223 *help! O, help* help   225 *of—O, she's dead* of
226 *Who dead? Speak, man* Who, man? Speak   228 *poisoned; she
confesses* poisoned; she hath confessed   232 *judgment* justice   233
is this 'tis   252 *Edgar* Albany   258 *Howl, howl, howl* Howl, howl,
howl, howl   270 *you murderers* your murderous   274 *woman*
women   281 *brag* bragged   281 *and* or   283 *This is a dull sight.
Are* Are   289 *first* life   306 *no, no, no* no, no   308 *Thou'lt* O,
thou wilt   309 *Never, never, never, never, never* Never, never,
never   310 *sir* sir. o, o, o, o   316 *He* O, he   324 *Edgar* Albany
326 *hath* *have

*Details of the
Penguin Shakespeare and
other Penguin books
follow.*

THE PELICAN SHAKESPEARE

GENERAL EDITOR: ALFRED HARBAGE

Each play is presented as a separate volume, edited by a specialist. The text follows the most authoritative early version available, departing from its readings only where emendation is essential and justified.

AB1	MACBETH	*Edited by Alfred Harbage*
AB2	CORIOLANUS	*Harry Levin*
AB3	MEASURE FOR MEASURE	*R. C. Bald*
AB4	THE WINTER'S TALE	*Baldwin Maxwell*
AB5	HAMLET	*Willard Farnham*
AB6	RICHARD II	*Matthew Black*
AB7	HENRY IV: I	*M. A. Shaaber*
AB8	HENRY IV: II	*Allan Chester*
AB9	HENRY V	*Louis B. Wright and Virginia Freund*
AB10	OTHELLO	*Gerald E. Bentley*
AB11	TWELFTH NIGHT	*Charles Prouty*
AB12	MUCH ADO ABOUT NOTHING	*Josephine Waters Bennett*
AB13	TROILUS AND CRESSIDA	*Virgil Whitaker*
AB14	KING LEAR	*Alfred Harbage*
AB15	THE TEMPEST	*Northrop Frye*
AB16	RICHARD III	*G. Blakemore Evans*
AB17	AS YOU LIKE IT	*Ralph Sargent*
AB18	A MIDSUMMER NIGHT'S DREAM	*Madeleine Doran*
AB19	ROMEO AND JULIET	*John E. Hankins*
AB20	ANTONY AND CLEOPATRA	*Maynard Mack*
AB21	THE MERCHANT OF VENICE	*Brents Stirling*
AB22	JULIUS CAESAR	*S. F. Johnson*

In preparation

AB23	THE SONNETS	*Douglas Bush*
AB24	THE MERRY WIVES OF WINDSOR	*Fredson T. Bowers*

CHAUCER: THE CANTERBURY TALES

A Modern Version By
Nevill Coghill

This is the first English work to be included in the Penguin Classics series of modern translations. When it was published it was widely acclaimed as a means of bringing Chaucer to thousands of people who would never have read him otherwise. Reviewers were quick to realize that Mr Coghill, who is a fellow of Exeter College, Oxford, was the right person to have attempted the task.

Punch offered very high praise by saying ' . . . this translation will remain a beloved classic until the language changes again sufficiently to call for another renaissance'. *The Manchester Guardian* found that 'Mr Coghill has achieved his aim that his translation should be considered as a poem and not as a crib'. And the most enthusiastic welcome came from *The Times Educational Supplement* which said, 'Altogether Mr Coghill's achievement is remarkable. He has been almost consistently successful and his practice carries out his theory and intentions. The bland, humorous, observing, and courtly spirit that informs the original is somehow preserved in a different idiom'.

528 pages. $1.45

PLAYS BY BERNARD SHAW

*The following plays are published
in Penguin editions. Each play has the
complete text and the
author's preface.*

ANDROCLES AND THE LION

THE APPLE CART

ARMS AND THE MAN

CAESAR AND CLEOPATRA

CANDIDA

THE DEVIL'S DISCIPLE

THE DOCTOR'S DILEMMA

MAJOR BARBARA

MAN AND SUPERMAN

PYGMALION

SAINT JOAN

SEVEN ONE-ACT PLAYS

THE PELICAN GUIDE TO ENGLISH LITERATURE

EDITED BY BORIS FORD

The Age of Chaucer

Essays on individual writers and works, and an anthology of medieval texts which are otherwise virtually inaccessible to the general reader. A290

The Age of Shakespeare

Essays which consider in detail the plays of Shakespeare, and also essays on individual dramatists and poets and prose-writers – above all, Marlowe, Ben Jonson, and Bacon. A291

From Donne to Marvell

A series of essays dealing in detail with Donne, the poems of Ben Jonson, Herbert, and the devotional poets, the Cavalier poets, Milton, Marvell, Hobbes, Bunyan, and Cowley. A325

From Dryden to Johnson

This volume deals in detail with Dryden, Swift, Pope, Defoe, Richardson, Fielding, Smollett and Sterne, Goldsmith, Johnson, etc. There are also essays on Hogarth, and on 18th-century architecture and planning. A379

From Blake to Byron

Essays on Blake, Wordsworth, Coleridge, Keats, Shelley, Jane Austen, etc. A402

From Dickens to Hardy

The concluding volume includes essays on Dickens, Thackeray, Trollope, Tennyson, Browning, the Brontës, George Eliot, Carlyle, Ruskin, Arnold, Meredith, and Hardy as well as more general accounts of the social life, literature, and architecture of the time. A413

THE PELICAN BOOK OF
ENGLISH PROSE

EDITED BY KENNETH ALLOTT

A new and comprehensive anthology of prose prepared for the use and pleasure of the general reader and student. Each volume has an introduction to the prose styles of the time and biographical notes on the writers represented.

Elizabethan and Jacobean Prose: 1550–1620

Eighty writers are included, among them Shakespeare, Bacon, Raleigh, and Hooker, edited by Kenneth Muir. A360

Seventeenth Century Prose: 1620–1700

Selections from the professional essayists, from the scientists, and from diaries and memoirs, edited by Peter Ure. A361

Eighteenth Century Prose: 1700–1780

Extracts from Defoe, Horace Walpole, Swift, Fielding, Johnson, Gibbon, and many others, edited by Douglas Jefferson. A362

Prose of the Romantic Period: 1780–1830

Pictures of ordinary life and of the part played by religion and politics in this varied age, edited by Raymond Wright. A363

Victorian Prose: 1830–1880

Novelists, philosophers, poets, essayists, all the great nineteenth century names are included in this selection by Kenneth Allott. A364

THE PELICAN HISTORY
OF ENGLAND

While each volume is complete in itself, the whole series, edited by J. E. Morpurgo, has been planned to provide an intelligent and consecutive guide to the development of English society in all its aspects. The eight volumes are:

1. ROMAN BRITAIN
by Ian Richmond

2. THE BEGINNINGS OF ENGLISH SOCIETY
(from the Anglo-Saxon Invasion)
by Dorothy Whitelock

3. ENGLISH SOCIETY IN THE EARLY
MIDDLE AGES
by Doris Mary Stenton

4. ENGLAND IN THE LATE MIDDLE AGES
by A. R. Myers

5. TUDOR ENGLAND
by S. T. Bindoff

6. ENGLAND IN THE SEVENTEENTH CENTURY
by Maurice Ashley

7. ENGLAND IN THE EIGHTEENTH CENTURY
by J. H. Plumb

8. ENGLAND IN THE NINETEENTH CENTURY
by David Thomson

SPECIALLY WRITTEN FOR PENGUINS

THE GREEK MYTHS

Robert Graves

Not for over a century, since Smith's *Dictionary of Classical Mythology* first appeared, has the attempt been made to provide for the English reader a complete 'mythology,' in the sense of a retelling in modern terms of the Greek tales of gods and heroes. In the two volumes of this book Robert Graves, whose combination of classical scholarship and anthropological competence has already been so brilliantly demonstrated in *The White Goddess* and *Hercules, My Shipmate*, and his other novels, supplies the need. In nearly two hundred sections, it covers the Creation myths, the legends of the birth and lives of the great Olympians, the Theseus, Oedipus, and Heracles cycles, the Argonaut voyage, the tale of Troy, and much else.

All the scattered elements of each myth have been assembled into a harmonious narrative, which notes also many variants which may help to determine its ritual or historical meaning. Full references to the classical sources, and copious indexes, make the book as valuable to the scholar as to the general reader; and a full commentary to each myth explains and interprets the classical version in the light of to-day's archaeological and anthropological knowledge. 1026, 1027

Two volumes: $1.25 each